FAITH FOR THE JOURNEY

Youth Explore the Confession of Faith

Ann Weber Becker

Scottdale, Pennsylvania
Newton, Kansas
Waterloo, Ontario
Winnipeg, Manitoba

Faith & Life
Resources

Printed in the United States of America
2345   02010099

International Standard Book Number 0-87303-313-2

Editorial direction for Faith & Life Press by Susan E. Janzen; copyediting by Mary L. Gaeddert; design by Jim L. Friesen; printing by Mennonite Press.

Contents

"Come and see ..."

a Samaritan woman
John 4:29

to Luke and Joel
and others just beginning the journey

Acknowledgments

This resource did not take shape overnight, nor did it evolve in the isolation of one person's study. I am indebted to many who assisted, shaped, and encouraged along the way.

I am grateful to the seven persons who gathered in Chicago (in severe weather, no less) to dream about what an Anabaptist catechetical resource for youth might look like. The vision and enthusiasm of Susan Janzen, Janeen Bertsche Johnson, Abe Bergen, King Hung Wan, Ingrid Schultz, Helmut Harder, and Mike Peak launched this project and sustained it in later stages.

For her ongoing support, wisdom, and carefulness, editor Susan Janzen has my gratitude.

I thank Abe Bergen, Lois Barrett, and Helmut Harder for their critiques of the paraphrases of the *Confession of Faith in a Mennonite Perspective* articles—Abe with an eye to accessibility for youth; Lois and Helmut alert to preserving the intent of the original articles.

I am indebted to a group of pastors and youth who frequently gathered with me to study drafts of chapters and share their counsel: Allan Rudy-Froese and Ben Janzen of Rockway Mennonite Church, Kitchener; Julie Ellison and Allison Reibling of Tavistock Mennonite Church; and Dave Tiessen and Hannah Hastings of Mannheim Mennonite Church, all of Ontario. Humor and hallowed moments were at home in these meetings, which contributed many splendid insights and ideas. My sincere thanks.

Sample chapters were tested and critiqued in a variety of settings far from the maple trees of Ontario. The wisdom of these groups molded not only the chapters in question but also the resource in its entirety. With appreciation, I thank Ingrid Schultz, Kathy Roth, and youth from Comunidad de Fe, Chicago, Illinois; Doug Kaufman and youth from Forest Hills Mennonite Church, Leola, Pennsylvania; John Kroeker and youth from First Mennonite Church, Mountain Lake, Minnesota; and Susan Kennel Harrison and youth from Evanston Mennonite Church, Evanston, Illinois.

Support of various kinds came from many different directions. In Women's Group friends Melissa Miller and Esther Epp-Tiessen I found, as always, trusted soul mates and sage encouragement from others familiar with the angst of committing words to paper. From Mom and Dad (Marg and Lew) Weber, Dennis and Luann Good Gingrich, and Friday morning Our Place staff, Joel received loving attention and creative play, and I received some extra time to write. When the children got sick the week of my deadline, Merri Kraemer Slagell graciously stepped in to help. Sisters and brothers at Mannheim Mennonite Church, Mom and Dad (Ardys and Palmer) Becker, Miriam Hellinga, Sing Thing friends, Kitchener Public Library's As You Like It Café staff, and Simeon Street neighbors rarely missed an opportunity to ask how things were going. And not to be missed are the youth of First Mennonite Church, Kitchener, with whom I journeyed in settings like those envisioned for this resource. Thanks to all.

Then there is Eleanor Snyder. With Eleanor's office and my home only blocks apart, meeting to brainstorm ideas for exercises was all too handy. Eleanor's support for this project and the writer behind it flowed almost as freely as the coffee. Her expertise and unflagging creativity have left their marks on almost every chapter. Eleanor, grateful thanks.

Finally, with a full heart, I thank my children, Luke and Joel, whose love and wonder have made the hand of God more visible to me than any theological treatise. And to my husband, Byron, my thanks—for unwavering commitment to carving out protected blocks of writing time, for competent technical support, and for introducing me to the beauty of backpacks. Most of all, thanks for sharing this chapter of the journey with me.

May the fruits of our labors be blessed. Shalom.

Introduction for Leaders

Throughout time, God's people have embarked on journeys that have deepened their faith. Who has not, at some point, known the shoes of Abram or Sarai, hearing God's urging to take leave of the familiar on the strength of a promise? Whether the journey takes us to another land or around the corner is of little consequence. Trusting God to guide, the journey may be long or short, direct or circuitous, rugged or easy. But for all who set out, there is the promise of a blessing.

During adolescence, many youth discover a desire to explore their growing faith. This resource was created with the hope of supporting youth and their pastors and other leaders in this exploration. Some may turn to it in a catechism setting when youth are considering a formal commitment to Christ and the church. It may also be useful for Sunday school, youth retreats, or for conversations within the family or between youth and their mentors. The format also lends itself to individual study.

Theological Grounding

This resource contains one chapter for each of the articles in the *Confession of Faith in a Mennonite Perspective*. Each chapter contains a biblical text relating to its theme. In choosing texts, preference was given to biblical narratives, as stories are often more readily understood by youth. Each chapter also contains a summary of an article from the Confession, rewritten or paraphrased, with an eye for making its content more accessible to youth.

While a paraphrase will naturally lead to embellishments in some cases and distillations in others, every effort was made to preserve the theological intent of each article. To assist in this regard, the rewritten summaries were read and critiqued by two members of the Confession of Faith Committee: Helmut Harder (co-chair) and Lois Barrett (writer). Occasionally material is quoted directly from the Confession of Faith, indicated with quotation marks. See the Opening Session (p. 1) for a brief explanation of the background of the *Confession of Faith in a Mennonite Perspective*.

Using the Sessions

Each chapter is written in such a way that it may be used by either an individual or a group. An individual may use this book as an interactive journal by working through the exercises and readings. A group leader will find instructions in the sidebars in the margins of the pages to assist in transforming the written exercises into a group experience of about forty-five to fifty minutes' duration. When this book is used in a group setting, it should support the group experience without being the focus of it. For instance, a session should not begin with the words "Please turn to page ...." Instead, create an active learning environment, and refer youth to the book when needed.

Each session is presented in a five-part format. **Focus** invites youth into the session's topic by connecting with some element of their life experience. **Explore** probes the topic a little deeper, exploring a range of possibilities. **Digging Deeper** offers the opportunity to look at a relevant Scripture text and the Confession of Faith summary. **Respond** invites youth to begin to integrate into their own journeys what they have explored in the session. **Closing** contains an idea for a group prayer as well as an opportunity for reflective journaling about memorable ideas, surprises that arose, questions that remain, etc. This journaling time may become part of the group session, or it may work better to send it home with youth to do on their own.

Sometimes more than one exercise is offered for the **Explore**, **Study**, and **Respond** parts of the session. While your group may have time to do all of the exercises that are offered, this format gives you the flexibility to build the session around the needs and interests of the group. If you do need to drop exercises, try to keep one from each of the five parts of the session. Answers to the questions in some of the exercises are found in Appendix 1.

You may wish to experience all the sessions in their printed order, in a different order, or select a smaller grouping from these twenty-six sessions. Each chapter was written to be freestanding. Chapters are not of uniform length, but they follow the same format throughout.

As with any curriculum, use these materials as a guide. You may use few, if any, of the sessions exactly as outlined, given the issues and circumstances unique to your group. Adapt freely (but do remember that people learn in different ways) and aim to hit a variety of styles in every session. Be alert for how your preferred style of learning influences what you choose to use or drop. Remember too that "fun" often enhances learning.

You, the Leader

If the youth in your group are on a journey, then you are their guide. They will look to you for direction and guidance. They will trust you. Recognize that you are stepping into a role of great responsibility and proceed as any experienced mountain guide would: with care and confidence. Youth will likely welcome hearing about your past adventures and experiences. Before each session, think through how the beliefs articulated in the Confession of Faith have found expression in your life.

If at some point you intend to extend an invitation to youth to voice their desire to follow Christ, think through carefully how and when this will happen. Share your plan with the youth, so they will not be taken by surprise. This might best be done individually. Consider meeting with each youth at some point to check in. Chapter 8, "Salvation," includes an optional opportunity to invite commitment (of course, this opportunity exists anytime). The Closing Session is written in a way that celebrates the experiences that all have had on this journey. A call to commitment is not included here since the emphasis in this session is on the group, not the individual.

Materials

Make sure that each youth has their own Bible (in a translation that is accessible to them) and their own copy of this book. Each person should also have a loose-leaf scrapbook (a three-ring binder with blank and lined paper, and dividers if you wish) to collect work they will produce on their journey. A personal copy of *Confession of Faith in a Mennonite Perspective* (Scottdale, Pennsylvania, and Waterloo, Ontario: Herald Press, 1995) could be a useful resource for this part of the journey and a helpful bridge to future journeys. Pencils, pens, a highlighter, and colored markers will also be required.

The Opening Session suggests purchasing one backpack per person. This is an added expense, but worth the investment when you consider the frustration it will save (when everything is together in one place, pieces are harder to forget). Of equal significance, the backpack will underscore the "journey" motif, signal that this is a journey to be taken seriously, and serve as a reminder of your support and the support of the congregation. Consider publicly presenting the backpack to youth in your worship hour and praying for them as they begin. Back-to-school specials or other seasonal sales often offer backpacks at reasonable prices.

Occasional reference is made to hymns or prayers in the most recent hymnal for the Church of the Brethren, Mennonite Church, and General Conference Mennonite Church: *Hymnal: A Worship Book* (Newton, Kansas: Faith & Life Press, 1992). If your congregation uses another hymnal or songbook, please substitute this book in its place. The intent is to draw youth into the worship songbook of your congregation.

Appendix 2 contains lists of other materials needed for each session. If the session suggests inviting a guest, this is also noted in Appendix 2. Appendix 3 gives more details about guests, and notes other special events for which you'll need to plan ahead.

Godspeed

May this journey of faith be meaningful and memorable for your students—and for you. Journey well.

OPENING SESSION

Welcome

Welcome to an exciting time in your life! You are invited to pick up your backpack and embark on a journey of faith. This is not the first leg of your journey, to be sure, but another portion of the trip. On this journey you may meet up with much that is familiar. You may also encounter new experiences. Journeys are exciting because they often expand our horizons by showing us new sights and helping us see old sights with new eyes.

Warm Up

Before you begin, take a moment to take stock. Why are you here, now, ready to embark on this journey?

Is there anything in your backpack you would like to take out and leave here at the beginning of the trail? Is there any extra baggage you don't want to carry with you the whole trip?

Equipment

What equipment will you need for this journey?:

- this book (it will serve as your map; you can use it yourself or in a group, using the instructions in the sidebar to the left)
- Bible (you will open it often)
- scrapbook (a three-ring binder with blank and lined paper, and dividers if you wish)
- pencils, pens, markers
- a copy of *Confession of Faith in a Mennonite Perspective* (see below)
- other stuff (some chapters call for special materials like clay, magazines, food, and so on—you will discover these as you go)

What is *Confession of Faith in a Mennonite Perspective*? Mennonite groups have sometimes taken the trouble to put down in writing what they

Get to know each other better. Invite each person in turn to share three things about themselves (hobbies, things that have happened to them, etc.). Two of these things will be true. One will be false. The rest of the group guesses which item is the "false" one. Even people who know each other well can have fun playing this game. If the people in your group do not know each other well, extend the "Welcome" section with other meaningful get-acquainted activites. If the people in your group know each other well, you may find this session too short. If so, consider moving ahead into "God" or one of the other chapters at your first meeting.

Have a backpack in the middle of your group as a visual aid while youth answer the warm up questions. Have the "equipment" listed in the next exercise in the backpack. If you ask youth to share their responses, be sure to participate yourself.

Take these items out of the backpack as you refer to them. Provide each youth with a copy of this book, a loose-leaf scrapbook as described, a copy of **Confession of Faith in a Mennonite Perspective**, and a pencil, pen, and even a pack of markers. Make sure everyone has a Bible. A very nice touch: give each youth a backpack for this important equipment on this significant journey! A creative touch: draw up the schedule for your class in the form of a map, showing "where you will be" on certain dates.

Help youth identify who they would like to have in this role of mentor/prayer partner. It may be helpful for you to approach the people they name to secure their commitment and clarify expectations. Invite the group to pray for each other.

Invite youth to write down their hopes and goals. Distribute envelopes. Instruct them to put the paper in the envelope, seal it, and write their names on the outside. Collect the sealed envelopes and save for the Closing Session (p. 107).

believe. Hundreds of years ago, a group of Anabaptists, forerunners of Mennonites, wrote down the basics of their beliefs in what is now known as the Schleitheim Articles of 1527. Since then, Mennonites have produced dozens of confessions of faith. Most recently, two Mennonite groups in North America (the Mennonite Church and the General Conference Mennonite Church) adopted *Confession of Faith in a Mennonite Perspective*.

This Confession of Faith was affirmed in 1995, but it was being developed many years before that. For ten years, people across the church studied and fine-tuned the material in the Confession. A committee pulled it all together, but hundreds, even thousands of people helped to shape the Confession by discussing drafts of the articles in Sunday school classes, writing letters to the committee, or sharing their wisdom in other ways.

Every chapter in this book has a summary of an article from *Confession of Faith in a Mennonite Perspective*. Note that this is not the original article, but a rewritten summary of the article. When more than a phrase or sentence is borrowed from the Confession of Faith, the borrowed text is marked with quotation marks. Sometimes you may wish to refer to the original Confession for more detail, Scripture references, and the background information in the commentary for each article.

Traveling Companions

Who will accompany you on this journey?

Find someone who will meet with you regularly to support you and share from their faith experience with you. This person should also commit to pray for you regularly. Who will this person be?

If you are meeting with others, make a commitment to pray for each other along the way.

Finally, don't forget your parents, pastor, youth leaders, and others who would like to be of assistance to you.

Destination

At the end of this journey, where do you hope to be? What are your hopes for what will happen? Do you have specific goals for this experience? Fill in at least two of the blanks below:

I hope to _____

I plan to _____

I wish _____

I aim to _____

Closing

Write a prayer to God as you prepare to set out on this journey. Listen for God's response to your prayer—now and in the coming week.

Closing prayer: Invite God's presence and guidance in the journey you are about to undertake. Sit in a circle with the backpack in the center as a visual symbol of your journey. In prayer, pass the backpack around the circle, praying for each person in turn as they hold the backpack. As this is your first session, be prepared to take the lead throughout, especially opening and closing the prayer.

1 GOD

Focus

How do we know what God is like? Sometimes the Bible gives us word pictures (or images) to help us begin to understand part of what God is like. Which of the following are images of God found in the Bible? Circle those that are.

rock	**water**	**shield**
shepherd	**mother**	**father**
ruler	**judge**	**mother bear**

Bring objects to class to represent these images. For instance, bring a rock, a pitcher of water, etc. Ask youth to sort the objects into two piles: those things that represent biblical images of God and those that don't. Answers are in Appendix 1.

Explore

No one word picture will ever give us a complete understanding of God. When I pick up a rock from my garden, I will not hold it up to you and say, "God is exactly like this." But I may give you the rock and ask you if the rock helps you call to mind a small part of what God is like.

Invite youth to choose one object from the collection and tell the group how this thing is and is not like God.

Choose one image from the list above. Write this image in the blanks below and complete the sentences.

God is like a _____, because God…

God is *not* like a _____, because God…

Do this exercise again, with an image that is especially helpful to you. When you think about God, what images come to mind? Choose one image and think about it for a moment. How does this image help remind you of God or help you understand God?

Invite youth to share their images with each other.

God is like _____, because God…

God is *not* like _____, because God…

Digging Deeper

Read these biblical texts and the Confession of Faith Summary. As you read, look for possible responses to these questions: How may we know God? How may we come close to God?

Psalm 52:8-9

"I am like a green olive tree in the house of God.
I trust in the steadfast love of God forever and ever.
I will thank you forever, because of what you have done.
In the presence of the faithful I will proclaim your name, for it is good."

1 John 4:8

"Whoever does not love does not know God, for God is love."

Confession of Faith Summary

"We believe that God exists and is pleased with all who draw near by faith." Throughout time, God has called forth a people of faith to worship, witness, and love. This people began with Abraham and Sarah. Thanks to the faithfulness of Jesus, this people extends to us when the Holy Spirit moves us to confess Jesus as Savior and Lord.

We believe that God is much more than we will ever be able to comprehend or understand. At the same time, we believe that "God has spoken to humanity and related to us in many" ways. So it is that we speak with both humility and confidence about knowing God. We believe that God has spoken above all in Jesus. Through Jesus we see most clearly who God is and what God is like.

"God's awesome glory and enduring compassion are perfect in holy love. God's sovereign power and unending mercy are perfect in almighty love. God's knowledge of all things and care for creation are perfect in preserving love. God's abounding grace and wrath against sinfulness are perfect in righteous love. God's readiness to forgive and power to transform are perfect in redemptive love. God's unlimited justice and continuing patience with humankind are perfect in suffering love. God's infinite freedom and constant self-giving are perfect in faithful love."

God is awesome! Glory to God!

Respond 1

If a friend asked you, "How do you know God?" or "How does God get through to you?" what would you say? Choose the response(s) below that you would most likely use. Are there any listed here that you would definitely not use?

Take turns verbalizing the response each would choose. Youth may wish to change words to make their response their own. Perhaps someone has a response that is not listed here. Are there any responses they are not comfortable with? In closing, you may wish to refer back to material in the Confession of Faith Summary.

"God speaks to me most clearly when I'm in the woods, or under a starry sky, or somewhere else where I'm in touch with God's creation."

"I hear God through the Bible. Sometimes a light goes on when I'm reading and I understand something better. But often it's things in my head from what I've read before that bubble back and guide me."

"I look to Jesus as an important example of what God is like. After all, Jesus is God in human form."

"I think Jesus is the clearest example, but there are people before and since that were so closely connected to God, they can help us know God. I'm thinking of people like Abraham and Sarah, the prophet Jeremiah, the apostle Paul, Menno Simons, Martin Luther King Jr., and Mother Teresa."

"I just think. I think about how creation happened, or how God can be everywhere at once, or why there is suffering in the world. When I think hard about things like these, God gets through to me."

"I look around me to the people in my church. Watching how they live their lives, listening to what they say, and worshiping together all help me connect with God and understand God better."

"I pay attention to current events in the world. God led the Israelites out of Egypt, and I think God is still active in our time, freeing people from oppression and helping them find justice."

Adapted from Basic Beliefs *by Sue Clemmer Steiner,*
Foundation Series for Youth, Year 4, Quarter 4, Unit A

Respond 2

Love comes in many different forms. When a parent gives a young child eyedrops to clear up an infection, it is difficult for the child to understand that the parent is acting out of love! Receiving presents at Christmastime is much easier to link with love, but this is just one more expression of love, like the eyedrops. When the Scriptures testify that "God is love," we might expect that God will express this love in a variety of ways—but love is always at the heart. God can even bring together qualities that might seem to us to be contradictory.

Write your name in the blanks in the heart on the top. Read these words as if God is saying them directly to you. What meaning does this message have for you? Write your response to God in the heart on the bottom.

God's words to me:

But now thus says the Lord,
he who created you, _____,
he who formed you, _____:
Do not fear, for I have redeemed you;
I have called you by name,
you are mine ..
you are precious in
my sight, and honored,
and I love you ....

Isaiah 43:1, 4a

My response to God:

Respond 3

God created YOU, formed YOU, and loves YOU! Create something that reminds you of God's love. Use pipe cleaners, chenille wire, clay, or anything else you can touch and mold. Put your creation someplace where you will see it often as a reminder of God's love for you and the world.

Closing

Record your personal response to this chapter. What has made an impression on you? What will you remember most? Was anything exciting? What seems most important? Any surprises? Do questions remain? Record your personal response in whatever form you wish: sentences, points, poetry, pictures, music, prayer.

God and Me

Distribute chenille wire (long, fuzzy "pipe cleaners" that come in a variety of colors). Invite youth to create a visual reminder of God's love. Share with each other what you created.

Closing prayer: Stand in a circle, holding hands, ready to go around the circle taking turns completing the sentence "I love you God, because _____." This sentence may be completed silently or audibly. When the first person is finished, he or she should squeeze the hand of the person on the left, and that person continues. As leader, open and close this prayer time.

2 JESUS CHRIST

Focus

Imagine that you have been appointed God's representative on earth for one year. You have twelve months to make God more real to the world in your time and place. How will you live out that role? What will you do with your life?

Give time to respond to this question individually, then share responses in pairs.

Explore

Jesus was God's representative on earth. Recall what you have experienced and learned about Jesus throughout your life. How would you describe Jesus? Lean back, and recall songs, hymns, pictures, Bible stories, lessons from teachers, conversations with parents and friends, and so on. Make a list of the qualities and characteristics you associate with Jesus.

Work in pairs or small groups. "Kindness" and "courage" are two examples of qualities that many people associate with Jesus.

Digging Deeper 1

Read Philippians 2:5-8 (part of a hymn about Jesus from the early church) and the Confession of Faith Summary about Jesus. As you read, look for more characteristics of Jesus that you could add to the list you just made.

Philippians 2:5-8

"Let the same mind be in you that was in Christ Jesus,
   who, though he was in the form of God,
      did not regard equality with God
      as something to be exploited,
   but emptied himself,
      taking the form of a slave,
      being born in human likeness.

And being found in human form,
  he humbled himself
  and became obedient to the point of death—
  even death on a cross."

Confession of Faith Summary

We believe in Jesus Christ, the Word of God become flesh. After a long wait, God sent Jesus into the world to give us a clear picture of who God is, who we are, and how we can grow closer to God. Jesus delivered us from the powers of sin and evil.

We can learn to know Jesus from many different angles. "We confess Jesus as the Christ, the Messiah, through whom God has prepared the new covenant for all peoples." Jesus was a prophet; he called everyone to repent. Jesus was a teacher. He knew how to live his life in a way that was pleasing to God. He is a good example for us to follow. Jesus was a faithful high priest. Like a high priest of his day, he helped people connect with God, but he helped people connect once and for all. Jesus was a king—but a king that was full of surprises. Who ever heard of a powerful king doing the job of a servant, enduring torture when he could have put a stop to it, or loving the people who were hurting him? Yet in his wisdom, these were things that Jesus chose to do.

"We accept Jesus Christ as the Savior of the world." Jesus proclaimed forgiveness and peace with both his words and his actions. He began a new community of faith by calling disciples to follow him and learn from him. He loved his enemies, even in his suffering. "In the shedding of his blood on the cross, Jesus offered up his life to the Father, bore the sins of all, and reconciled us to God." But Jesus' death was not the last word. God defeated the powers of death and evil, and brought Jesus back to life.

"We acknowledge Jesus as the only Son of God." Jesus knows what it is like to be human like us, AND divine like God. Because he was fully human, Jesus knows what it is like to face all the temptations that we face. But because he faced all these temptations without sin, he is a model human being for us to follow. Because Jesus was fully divine, we can look to him to better understand God, for God dwelled in Jesus.

We believe that the church is the body of Christ, with Jesus as its head. In this way, we are "in Christ" when we are members of the church. When we are part of the church, Christ dwells in us—you cannot get much closer than that! This close relationship helps the church carry on Jesus' ministry of mercy, justice, and peace in a broken world.

We not only respect and learn about Jesus, we also worship him. We believe that Jesus is our Lord and the not-yet-recognized Lord of the whole world. We can look forward to the time when he will come again, and all humanity will be held up to his example. Then he will finally be acknowledged Lord of all and will reign forever and ever.

Digging Deeper 2

Jesus filled many different roles in his life and ministry. Four of these are listed below. Jot down a few words to remind you what each one means. (Don't be afraid to consult a teacher or a reference book if you need to.) Now ask yourself, "Which role would I choose as the most important part of Jesus?" Rank the most important as 1, the next most important as 2, and so on. There are no right answers here. The point is, what would *you* choose?

Ranking	Role	"What is it?"	References
_____	prophet	_____	Matthew 21:11
_____	teacher	_____	John 3:2
_____	priest	_____	Hebrews 4:14, 15
_____	king	_____	Luke 19:38

What did you choose as #1 (most important)? Why?

What did you choose as #4 (least important)? Why?

Take a poll of the class to do a group ranking by adding scores for each role. The most important will have the lowest score. Share your descriptions with each other. See Commentary #2 in "Confession of Faith in a Mennonite Perspective" for the Old Testament roots of these roles.

Respond 1

If Christ were to walk beside you for a week, where would you want to take him? Are there places Christ could go that would help him better understand you? Are there places you could go that would help you better understand him? Where would you go? Why?

Share responses to these questions in pairs.

Respond 2

You have been asked to introduce Jesus in your worship service. Based on all that you have discovered about Jesus, how will you introduce him? Figure out not only what you want to say but also how you will say it, who will be involved, when it should happen in the service, and so on. If this were for real, what a tremendous opportunity this would be! What will you make of it?

Introductions may be worked at individually or in pairs. Be sure to save time to actually do the introductions. Have microphones on hand as props.

Closing prayer: Lead a prayer using the sentence "Jesus, you are _____," drawing on the list of qualities youth identified in Explore. Invite youth to complete the sentence as many times as they wish. Each time, respond with the refrain "Thank you, God, for Jesus."

Closing

Record your personal response to this chapter. What has made an impression on you? What will you remember most? Was anything exciting? What seems most important? Any surprises? Do questions remain? Record your personal response in whatever form you wish: sentences, points, poetry, pictures, music, prayer.

Jesus Christ and Me

3 HOLY SPIRIT

Focus

What kind of fuel have you used today? What appliances and machines have you used or have others used for you? How have you traveled around? Has your space been heated or cooled by anything? What has your body used for fuel? As you think about your day, circle all the different kinds of fuel you have used and add more if you need:

gasoline   **oil**   **electricity**
coal   **food**   **solar power**
wind   **kerosene**   **propane**

Start by asking what fuel people used to get to the church or wherever you are meeting.

Explore

Have you ever thought of the Holy Spirit as "fuel"—not the kind of fuel that powers cars or compact disc players, but a "fuel" that powers the church? When a car speeds down the highway at 100 kilometers per hour, we see evidence of the fuel in its gas tank. When people in a congregation come together to support each other in hard times (for example), we see evidence of the Holy Spirit. How do you see the Holy Spirit at work?

Record everyone's ideas on a chalkboard or posterboard.

Digging Deeper 1

Read the text from Ezekiel and the Confession of Faith Summary. Highlight or underline all the things that the Spirit does.

Ezekiel 36:26-28

"A new heart I will give you, and a new spirit I will put within you; and I will remove from your body the heart of stone and give you a heart of flesh. I will put my spirit within you, and make you follow my statutes and be

Have a large piece of fabric and fabric paints (or permanent markers) available. As the group identifies the verbs or action words related to the Holy Spirit, write them on the fabric with the fabric paint. Do not list them in neat lines and columns. "Scrawl" them in a helter-skelter way to communicate the energy and restlessness of the Spirit. Later, mount it outside like a flag. Watch the wind blow it! Remember the Holy Spirit "blowing" in our midst (John 3:8).

careful to observe my ordinances. Then you shall live in the land that I gave to your ancestors; and you shall be my people, and I will be your God."

Confession of Faith Summary

We believe that the Spirit of God has been active through all time. The world was created through the Spirit of God. Writers of Scripture were inspired. People were enabled to follow God's law. Jesus was filled with the Holy Spirit, proclaiming good news, healing the sick, and even accepting death. By the power of the Holy Spirit he was raised from the dead.

At Pentecost, God began to pour out the Spirit to all corners of the earth. The church was gathered up from people of many nations. The church became a home for the Holy Spirit—a dwelling place where the Spirit can move and live. The guidance of the Spirit leads the church to unity. The gifts of the Spirit empower Christians to live and minister in God's way.

When we are aware of the Spirit working in our lives, Scripture urges us to be open to the Spirit's movement, not resisting or quenching the Spirit. The Holy Spirit dwells in each child of God. The Spirit seeks to bring us closer to God by teaching us, guiding us, reminding us of Jesus' word, empowering us to speak that word, and calling us to repentance. By water and the Spirit, we enter the family of God in a new way.

We believe that the Holy Spirit will continue to be active through all time. We can count on the Spirit to comfort us when we suffer, be present with us when persecution comes, help us live in Christian community, and ever so many other ways. The Holy Spirit even assures us that God's reign will come someday in a new heaven and a new earth.

Respond 1

Find a copy of *Hymnal: A Worship Book* or whatever hymnal your congregation uses. Look through hymns for more clues about how the Spirit is active in our world. Look up the "Proclaiming: Activity of the Spirit" section (#298-304). Also look up "Holy Spirit" in the topical index for more hymns in different sections of the hymnal. Note below any descriptions or phrases about the Spirit that are meaningful to you.

Add words or phrases from these hymns to the banner created in Digging Deeper 1. Consider singing one of these hymns together. Could you or someone in the group help lead with a guitar, piano, or confident singing voice? Or play a cassette tape of reflective music evoking the Holy Spirit.

Nut allergies are an increasing concern. Find out if there are any ingredients you should avoid before serving this snack to your group.

Respond 2

Find yourself some GORP ("good ole' raisins and peanuts"), or some other high-protein snack mix. This snack is good fuel while you are on the move hiking or traveling. While munching on the GORP, reflect on the observation that the GORP doesn't give our bodies fuel until we "access" it by eating it. How do we "access" the Holy Spirit?

Respond 3 (optional)

Choose one of the following activities or create a third idea that fits your interests:

Write a song about the Holy Spirit! Take a tune that you like and add new words. Or write a melody that communicates something about the Spirit to you. Or write your own words and the music to go with it.

Draw a picture that reflects the Holy Spirit's activity. Consider drawing a "before" and "after" picture that communicates how the Spirit might move in a given situation.

Add your creation to your scrapbook. Be sure to share your work with somebody!

Closing

Record your personal response to this chapter. What has made an impression on you? What will you remember most? Was anything exciting? What seems most important? Any surprises? Do questions remain? Record your personal response in whatever form you wish: sentences, points, poetry, pictures, music, prayer.

Holy Spirit and Me

Pray together for the Holy Spirit to enter the lives of your students in some of the ways they have identified in this session. Alternately, pray together #762 in Hymnal: A Worship Book:: "Come, Holy Spirit. Come as Holy Fire and burn in us...."

As you pray, hold your hands in front of you, palms upturned, in an attitude of invitation to the Spirit.

4 SCRIPTURE

Focus

Have you come across interesting "Bible bits" like these? Which of these are true and which are false?

T   F   1. Samson set three hundred foxes' tails on fire.

T   F   2. Trimming your beard was a no-no.

T   F   3. An angel assisted with an escape from jail.

T   F   4. Noah was 500 years old when his sons were born.

T   F   5. After making a speech, King Herod was eaten up by worms.

T   F   6. A fire burned stones.

T   F   7. The longest word in the Bible is "Mahershalalhashbaz."

T   F   8. There was a sea serpent at the bottom of a sea.

T   F   9. Three men in the Bible were named "Dodo."

For a lively start, divide the class into two teams. Pose the T/F statements, alternating between the teams. A correct answer earns a point. Award a bonus point if the team can also identify which book of the Bible this tidbit is from. (See the answers in Appendix 1.)

Explore

The exercise above is a lighthearted look at some little-known verses of the Bible, but learning the longest word in the Bible is probably not going to be an important part of your faith journey. Why is the Bible important? Look over the statements below and indicate how important each one is to you by using asterisks:

***	very important
**	pretty important
*	a little important
(none)	not important at all

Before class, write each of the statements on a different slip of paper. Distribute the slips evenly. Identify four areas of the floor or a bulletin board to correspond with the four degrees of importance. Each person in turn reads one of their statements and places it in the area they wish. Once finished, survey the results. Does the group have any statements to add?

The Bible is a book shared by Christians all around the world.

The Bible helps us worship God.

The Bible helps us make decisions.

The Bible helps us know God.

The Bible teaches us about Jesus.

The Bible is the Word of God.

The Bible is the book of the church.

The Bible tells us exactly what will happen in the future.
The Bible helps us know how to live.
The Bible connects us with people of faith who have gone before us.
The Bible guides our faith.
The Bible is a valuable piece of literature.
The Bible gives us hope for the future.

 # Digging Deeper 1

As you read the Confession of Faith Summary, look for more statements you could add to the list above about the importance of the Bible.

Confession of Faith Summary

We believe that God was at work for a long time bringing the Bible to be. God was involved in the process that resulted in the Old and New Testaments. People wrote the books of the Bible, but they did not do it on their own. They were guided and inspired by God through the Holy Spirit. What was the result? The Word of God written. In the pages of the Bible, we find what is needed for salvation, for guidance in faith and life, and for devotion to God.

God has spoken through faithful persons in many different ways over the centuries. Above all, God spoke through Jesus, the Word of God in human form. Jesus revealed the truth of God better than anyone else, before or since. Jesus continues to live through Scripture. God continues to speak through Scripture. We acknowledge Scripture as the fully reliable and trustworthy Word of God written in human language.

We turn to the Scriptures as a source of authority for our lives as Christians. Scripture is the standard for preaching and teaching about faith and life. It helps us distinguish truth from error, and good from evil. It undergirds our prayer and worship. Scripture also guides other ways we grow in faith. As they journey through life, Christians test their new insights and experiences in light of the Scriptures.

The Bible is the essential book of the church. The Holy Spirit can speak through the Bible to nurture our faith and guide the life of the church. In order to speak to us, the Bible must be opened! We commit ourselves to read the Bible, study it, and meditate on it. We will help the church interpret the Bible. We will look to the faith community to test our insights and understandings about the Bible. We will delight in the Bible!

Read the account below from Acts. With whom do you most identify: Philip or the Ethiopian? Why?

Acts 8:27b-35

"(An Ethiopian eunuch) had come to Jerusalem to worship and was returning home; seated in his chariot, he was reading the prophet Isaiah. Then the Spirit said to Philip, 'Go over to this chariot and join it.' So Philip ran up to it and heard him reading the prophet Isaiah. He asked, 'Do you understand what you are reading?' He replied, 'How can I, unless someone guides me?' And he invited Philip to get in and sit beside him. Now the passage of the scripture that he was reading was this: 'Like a sheep he was led to the slaughter, and like a lamb silent before its shearer, so he does not open his mouth. In his humiliation justice was denied him. Who can describe his generation? For his life is taken away from the earth.' The eunuch asked Philip, 'About whom, may I ask you, does the prophet say this, about himself or about someone else?' Then Philip began to speak, and starting with this scripture, he proclaimed to him the good news about Jesus."

Digging Deeper 2

The New Testament has four books that tell the life of Jesus: Matthew, Mark, Luke, and John. These books are called Gospels. Each Gospel is similar to the others, but also different. Each one has some material that none of the others have. (For instance, only Luke tells the story of the Prodigal Son.) Sometimes the same teaching or event is told by all four Gospels.

Compare the following texts that each relate the death of Jesus: Matthew 27:45-54; Mark 15:33-39; Luke 23:44-49; and John 19:28-30. In a page in your scrapbook, make four columns. Title each column with these references. Starting with Matthew, make a list down that column of all the points that appear significant from this text. Do the same for each of the others, writing similar points beside each other. When you are finished, compare the four accounts. Make at least three comments about what you see.

Digging Deeper 3
(Optional)

Sometimes we study the Bible in small portions, word by word. Sometimes we study the Bible in a more general way. Choose one of the Gospels (Matthew, Mark, Luke, or John), and read through it quickly, like you would read through a novel. If you like, choose one of the following themes, and trace it through the Gospel. You can make notes recording your findings in your journal scrapbook, or you could acquire a soft-cover Bible and use a highlighter as you read.

Choose one of these themes to guide your reading of one of the Gospels:

• How did people respond to Jesus?
• What kinds of feelings did Jesus have?
• How did Jesus use his power and authority?
• How did Jesus treat people on the fringes of Jewish society (i.e., children, women, sick, disabled, non-Jewish people)?

If you have at least four youth in your group, divide into four groups and assign a different Gospel text to each group. Let each group assign a "reporter" to tell the rest what they remember about the death of Jesus. Together, make a chart of your findings. If possible, have available a Synopsis of the Gospels. Using it for this exercise will speed up the process of comparing accounts.

Consider arranging a retreat time for the group to experience the Gospel of Mark. Divide the Gospel ahead of time, and ask each person to become familiar with their section. When you gather, dim the lights, light some candles, and simply tell Mark to each other all the way through.

Respond 1

Most Mennonites look to the Bible for guidance on what we believe and how we live. How do you see the Bible shaping your life and the life of your church?

Today, many other books and magazines vie for our attention, not to mention movies and the internet. Giving the Bible a place in our lives doesn't happen automatically. We need to make it happen. What would help you keep Bible study a priority or make it an important part of your life?

Respond 2

While there certainly is a place for studying the Bible by yourself and having solitary meditation on the Scriptures, studying the Bible with others is also important. What are the benefits of testing your interpretation of Scripture with others? What might some difficulties be, and how could those be worked at?

Studying the Bible with others

benefits	difficulties and possible solutions

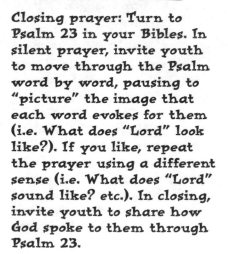

Closing prayer: Turn to Psalm 23 in your Bibles. In silent prayer, invite youth to move through the Psalm word by word, pausing to "picture" the image that each word evokes for them (i.e. What does "Lord" look like?). If you like, repeat the prayer using a different sense (i.e. What does "Lord" sound like? etc.). In closing, invite youth to share how God spoke to them through Psalm 23.

Closing

Record your personal response to this chapter. What has made an impression on you? What will you remember most? Was anything exciting? What seems most important? Any surprises? Do questions remain? Record your personal response in whatever form you wish: sentences, points, poetry, pictures, music, prayer.

Scripture and Me

5 CREATION AND DIVINE PROVIDENCE

Focus

Imagine that you were given the opportunity to be anything other than a person for a day. What would you be? Would you be a certain bird or animal? Would you be part of an ocean? What about an object that someone has made? Would you be on earth or elsewhere in the universe? Identify 3-6 things that you would like to be.

> Ask youth to write one of their responses on a slip of paper. Collect the slips and put them in a basket. Have one person draw out a slip and guess who wrote that response. Once that person is identified, he or she joins the first person to make a "team" to again draw a slip and guess that person's identity. Continue until everyone is identified.

Explore 1

In your view, what is the most awesome piece of creation? Why?

> Share the answer to this question in pairs or triads.

Explore 2

Many people believe that God created the universe. Have you ever stopped to think why God might have done this? Why do you think God chose to create the universe? Check all the responses you agree with.

____ God created the universe by chance.
____ God was curious where it would all lead.
____ God was experimenting with power.
____ God was lonely.
____ God was bored and wanted some entertainment.
____ God wanted to express love and experience it.
____ other _____

> These exercises are intended to help youth identify ideas and impressions about creation that they have been exposed to in their lives. Let them share freely without evaluating at this point.

There are different ideas about how the universe came to be, and even whether God had anything to do with it. Take a pen and stroke out all the theories below that you do not agree with:

The "Big Bang" happened.
The universe evolved without God's help.
God caused the universe to evolve.
God created the world in six twenty-four-hour days.
The universe happened by chance.
Nobody knows.
Other _____.

Digging Deeper 1

The Bible starts at "the beginning," with God creating the heavens and the earth. The Confession of Faith states that we believe God created the universe. Read from Genesis and the article summary to find out why we believe God chose to create the universe.

Genesis 1:1-5

"In the beginning when God created the heavens and the earth, the earth was a formless void and darkness covered the face of the deep, while a wind from God swept over the face of the waters. Then God said, 'Let there be light'; and there was light. And God saw that the light was good; and God separated the light from the darkness. God called the light Day, and the darkness he called Night. And there was evening and there was morning, the first day."

Confession of Faith Summary

Have you ever heard someone ask the question "What is the meaning of life?" Sometimes it is asked without expecting an answer. But Christians believe there is a response to this question. First you need to do some thinking about how life came to be in the first place.

We believe that God chose to create the universe—and did so as an expression of love. Consider some of the alternatives. Did God need to create the universe? No, this was a choice freely made. Did God desire an elaborate toy for amusement? No, God created everything in love, not as an object to play with at whim.

The more we learn about creation, the more we learn about God's greatness and majesty. Whether exploring the mysteries of outer space or the mysteries of the atom, the conclusion is the same: God is awesome!

We believe that God continues to be involved with the universe. God is active, sustaining oceans and wildlife, molecules and galaxies. God is active, limiting the forces of sin and evil all around. God is active, saving human beings and the world from death and destruction. God is actively involved in both the changes in creation and in the things that stay the same.

Life is filled with meaning for Christians because living in God's world means participating with God in the unfolding of creation. It means respecting the creation that God so lovingly made. It means entrusting ourselves to God's care and keeping, even when things turn out differently than we think they should. It means honoring God above all else.

In light of this material, why do we believe that God chose to create the universe?

Digging Deeper 2

Psalm 104 praises God for an awesome creation. With your Bible, go outside and find a place where you have some privacy. Read Psalm 104 (aloud, go ahead!) as your song of praise to God.

Digging Deeper 3

Go on a walk by yourself. Even if you are walking someplace familiar, try to see the things around you with new eyes. Be aware of your sense of smell, of touch, of hearing, of sight, and maybe even taste (but never eat something when you don't know what it is!). Be in God's presence. Experience God's creation.

Respond 1

Create something, anything, as your response to God's work of creation. What you create may have something to do with how you are feeling: thankful, filled with awe, puzzled, excited, etc. Use whatever you like. You could use materials like clay, wood, or natural things. You could write a poem, a story, or a song. You might want to return to Psalm 104 and extend it by adding your own ideas. Roll up your sleeves and create a response to God.

Go outside and read this psalm responsively, or take turns reading verse by verse. It does not matter if you are in an urban or a rural setting. It does not matter if it is day or night. Wherever we are, whenever it is, we are surrounded by God's creation.

If your setting is safe for youth to be out alone, stay outside after reading Psalm 104 and scatter for 10-15 minutes for a solitary walk. If this is not possible in your setting, walk as a group, or encourage youth to do this later on their own. Rather than calling the group back together to talk about this experience, move directly into Respond 1.

Have on hand a variety of supplies and materials. Be sure that one of the things you have is clay or something like it (plasticine, modeling clay, or even homemade play dough). Create individually or in groups. Think through in advance where all this creative activity can happen. If this "isn't your thing," perhaps someone else in the congregation could gather materials and be available for this part of the session.

Closing prayer: Pray
together in silence,
listening for God. Open
with Psalm 136:26. Close
with Psalm 150:6.

Closing

Record your personal response to this chapter. What has
made an impression on you? What will you remember most?
Was anything exciting? What seems most important? Any
surprises? Do questions remain? Record your personal response in whatever
form you wish: sentences, points, poetry, pictures, music, prayer.

Creation and Me

6
THE CREATION AND CALLING OF HUMAN BEINGS

Focus

Grab a snack! While you are munching, sit back and think about what different ingredients went into what you are eating. Now think about where each ingredient came from. Try to trace each one back to its source (a plant or an animal) and, if possible, where that plant or animal would have come from. (One example is given.)

Serve a snack such as crackers, cheese, fruit, or something else reasonably nutritious. Follow the exercise where your snack leads you.

Ingredient	Source	Where it came from
flour	wheat	Saskatchewan or South Dakota

It may be easy to take for granted the world that God created, but we depend on it for our very existence.

Explore

If we depend on creation, how do we take care of it? How does God intend us to relate to animals, to the earth, to other humans, to God? Draw a picture or make some notes about how you think God desires us to relate to each of these.

Divide the class into two groups. Each group agrees on one idea for each of the four categories. Now enjoy a game of "Quick Draw." On a chalkboard or poster paper, one person from each team takes turns drawing their idea for the other team. The other team guesses their idea from their drawing.

Animals

Earth

Other humans

God

Keep the same groups you formed for Explore. In these groups, read the text and article, noting what they say about relationships.

Digging Deeper 1

Read the text from Genesis below and the Confession of Faith Summary. What strikes you about how God desires us to relate to different aspects of creation? Underline phrases or make notes in the margins with your ideas.

Genesis 1:26-28

"Then God said, 'Let us make humankind in our image, according to our likeness; and let them have dominion over the fish of the sea, and over the birds of the air, and over the cattle, and over all the wild animals of the earth, and over every creeping thing that creeps upon the earth.' So God created humankind in his image, in the image of God he created them; male and female he created them. God blessed them, and God said to them, 'Be fruitful and multiply, and fill the earth and subdue it; and have dominion over the fish of the sea and over the birds of the air and over every living thing that moves upon the earth.'"

Confession of Faith Summary

"Human beings were created good, in the image of God." While many other parts of creation are awesome and beautiful, only humans are made in God's image. We believe that in all of creation, human beings have a unique relationship with God. Stars are awe-inspiring, orca whales are beautiful, morning glories are charming, but it is you who are created in the image of God.

Being made in God's image has implications for how we relate to other parts of God's creation. We are to subdue and care for creation out of honor for God who created it. We have been blessed with the ability to respond faithfully to God. We can live in harmony with others. We can even engage in meaningful work and rest. Adam and Eve were equally and wonderfully made in God's image. From the beginning, God's will has been for men and women to live in loving and mutually helpful relationships with each other.

Like Adam and Eve, we make choices that disappoint God. We are grateful that God does not give up on us. God is patient with us. God preserves us through our learnings and our lousy moments. God also sent Jesus into the world to show us what it really means to be made in the image of God.

God is so faithfully present with us that God remains with us even through death. We believe that one day, everything will be made new. We can look forward to this day of salvation and redemption with hope.

Respond

In an ideal world, how would people relate to each other and to the world around them? Write up ten "Rules for Relating"—your own Ten Commandments for living with each other and the world! Just for fun, start each "Rule" with "Thou shalt," or "Thou shalt not"!

1.

2.

3.

4.

5.

6.

7.

8.

9.

10.

Give a few minutes for each person to get started on this individually. Then group into pairs. Remain in pairs until both people agree on a set of 10 rules. (There may need to be some give and take here.) If your group is large enough, regroup again by joining pairs into groups of four. Again, groups must agree on a common set of 10 rules before they part. Save time at the close of the exercise to debrief. Ask youth to reflect on how they related to each other during their deliberations. Did their group live up to the rules for relating that they were writing down? Any surprises?

Closing prayer: Pray to God for places in your experience and in the larger world where people are having trouble relating in ways God intended. In prayer, take turns voicing concerns out loud. As a group, pray silently for each concern.

Closing

Record your personal response to this chapter. What has made an impression on you? What will you remember most? Was anything exciting? What seems most important? Any surprises? Do questions remain? Record your personal response in whatever form you wish: sentences, points, poetry, pictures, music, prayer.

Creation, Human Beings, and Me

7 SIN

Focus

Sift through the following ideas about sin, and decide which ones you agree with and which ones you don't.

T	F	Sin makes us do things we don't want to do.
T	F	Sin keeps us from loving others.
T	F	Sin is a natural part of what it means to be human.
T	F	Sin breaks relationships with God and with others.
T	F	Sin is the garbage in life that we get sucked into.
T	F	There are demonic powers that whirl around us and try to grip us.
T	F	Obedience is hard.
T	F	We can't expect to be perfect—that's not us.
T	F	There are some sins that are too great for even God to forgive.
T	F	Everyone sins.

Write each of these phrases about sin on a different piece of paper. Post the papers around the room. Let youth circulate, marking their choice of T or F on each paper. If you like, make a quick tally of the "Three Top True's" and the "Three Top False's."

Explore

Do you see evidence of sin in our world? What do you think of when you think of "sin"? What actions would you call "sin"? Is there ever a time when something left undone is also sin? Take a moment to jot down your ideas and associations. Make as long a list as possible.

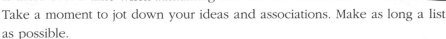

Look back over your list. Circle all of the items that are things one person would do by himself or herself. Underline all of the things that would be the result of the action of a group or organization. (Some of your items might fit into both of these categories. In that case, circle and underline that item.) Take a quick tally. Which has more, the individual actions (circles) or the group actions (underlines)? The Bible speaks to sins done by individuals and sins done by groups. If your list was almost all circles or almost all underlines, make the tally more even by adding to your list.

If your group is small, do this exercise all together. If your group is large, divide into groups of 3 or 4 per group.

Create a group collage on a large sheet of poster paper. Post the collage in a visible spot for the rest of the session.

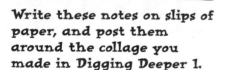

Digging Deeper 1

From newspapers or news magazines, clip out headlines, articles, and pictures that serve as evidence of sin. (Your clippings may reflect the power of "the four Ds": domination, division, destruction, and death.) Make a collage of these clippings on a page in your scrapbook.

Read the text from the book of Romans. Choose a short quotation from this text to stand as a headline for the collage you made. Add your headline with a bold marker right across the collage, or use a separate piece of paper and glue it onto the collage.

Romans 3:10-18

"... as it is written:
'There is no one who is righteous, not even one;
there is no one who has understanding,
    there is no one who seeks God.
All have turned aside, together they have become worthless;
    there is no one who shows kindness,
        there is not even one.'
'Their throats are opened graves;
    they use their tongues to deceive.'
'The venom of vipers is under their lips.'
    'Their mouths are full of cursing and bitterness.'
'Their feet are swift to shed blood;
    ruin and misery are in their paths,
and the way of peace they have not known.'
    'There is no fear of God before their eyes.'"

Digging Deeper 2

Write these notes on slips of paper, and post them around the collage you made in Digging Deeper 1.

Study the Confession of Faith Summary, looking for things that sin has the power to do. Jot these around your collage if there is room, or start a new page in your scrapbook and write them "graffiti-style."

Confession of Faith Summary

We believe that God trusts us with many choices, desiring that we turn toward God for worship and companionship. But like Adam and Eve, we sometimes choose to turn away from God and make gods of creation and of ourselves. This we call sin. Sometimes we choose on our own to do sinful things; sometimes we are part of a group that makes these choices. Sometimes we sin by choosing NOT to do something. Sin is like a poison that can contaminate our covenant with God. It can destroy good relationships. It can tempt us to use power selfishly or to act with violence. Sin is like a wall that can separate us from God.

Through sin, powers of evil remain active in humanity and in creation. Domination, division, destruction and death all thrive when we turn away from God. The more we sin, the more we become trapped in sin. By our sin, we open ourselves to the bondage of demonic powers. Sin can get in the way of people's efforts to do good and to know the truth.

By learning to recognize powers of evil at work in individuals, in groups, and in all of creation, we can see how sin can trap us. These powers can hold people captive. They can work through political, economic, social, and even religious systems to turn people away from doing good and walking in God's way.

But thanks be to God! God has not allowed powers of evil to reign supreme over creation. God has not left humanity without hope.

Respond 1

Do you have a perfection complex? Do you live your life striving to be perfect? (After all, Jesus was perfect, and we're supposed to pattern ourselves after Jesus, right?) On the other hand, do you ignore your sins or explain them away?

Trying to be perfect is a heavy burden—and likely not one that we were meant to bear. After all, the prayer that Jesus taught us to pray (the Lord's Prayer) asks God to "forgive us our sins," which probably means God expects us to have some!

The key is what we do with the things that separate us from God. Here's your chance to look at your life straight on, in the spotlight. Answer any of the following questions that speak to you.

What in my life am I hiding from others?

What do I need to come clean on?

What am I struggling to leave behind?

Why do I feel powerless and trapped?

Is there anything about my life I would feel embarrassed about if Jesus walked beside me for a day?

Write a prayer to God in which you confess your sin and ask for forgiveness. Pray for the humility to learn from mistakes and for the courage to move on.

Help everyone find a solitary corner for this activity to be done individually. When you regroup, remind them that you are available after class (or whenever) to talk with them if needed. When you talk with youth, be aware of the potential power of guilt and shame in their lives. Consider the difference between "good" guilt and "bad" guilt. Good guilt pricks our consciences and helps us recognize sin. On the other hand, childhood experiences, normally developing bodies, or other experiences beyond young people's control can result in bad guilt that can drag them down and keep them from experiencing shalom. Explore how the unnecessary burden of bad guilt might be shed, and encourage how the messages of good guilt might be taken seriously. Close this exercise by reciting the Lord's Prayer together.

Read aloud Mark 10:46-52.
In a prayerful mood, pose
the questions asked in this
exercise. Do not require
youth to respond verbally.

Respond 2

Once during Jesus' travels, he and his disciples were on their way out of Jericho. They were not alone; a large crowd was also on the road out of Jericho that day. A blind beggar was sitting by the roadside. He called out to Jesus. Many ordered him to be quiet, but he persisted. When Jesus heard his cry, he stopped, and asked that the blind man be brought to him.

Look up the story of Jesus and the blind beggar in Mark 10:46-52. Put yourself "in the shoes" of the blind beggar. Imagine for a moment that your blindness is not a result of physical problems, but caused by an invisible wall that surrounds you. The wall lets no light through and separates you from Jesus. How do you feel? What do you want? What do you cry out to Jesus as he approaches?

In the Gospel of Mark, Jesus says to the blind beggar, "Go; your faith has made you well" (Mark 10:52). What does Jesus say to you?

Closing prayer: Invite youth
to offer the prayers
composed at the end of
Respond 1. Sing "Lord, listen
to your children" (Hymnal:
A Worship Book, #353),
alternating with the spoken
prayers. Close with an
affirmation of God's power
over evil; God has not left
us without hope. Then sing
#353 once more.

Closing

Record your personal response to this chapter. What has made an impression on you? What will you remember most? Was anything exciting? What seems most important? Any surprises? Do questions remain? Record your personal response in whatever form you wish: sentences, points, poetry, pictures, music, prayer.

Sin and Me

8 SALVATION

Focus

What associations do you have with the word *salvation*? Answer this question: When I hear the word *salvation*, I feel ...

Give youth a few moments to identify a word or phrase in response. Invite them to voice their responses "popcorn" style.

Explore

The Bible describes salvation in a variety of ways. Decide which ones you can identify with, and check them. Being saved is like ...

____ being a prisoner and then being set free

____ living in darkness and then seeing the light

____ being guilty and then experiencing forgiveness

____ having a huge debt and then finding out it's paid

____ being dead and then coming alive

____ being confused and then getting things straightened out

____ being rejected and then being accepted

____ being lost and then being found

____ being an enemy and then a friend

____ having no meaning and purpose and then finding a reason to live

From "Discipleship Daily #1" by Don and Dorothy Friesen, Foundation Series for Youth, Year 4, Quarter 1, Unit A

Before class, write each of these descriptions on a slip of paper. Place them in a basket. Pass the basket around the circle. Invite each person to draw a slip and read the description. If anyone in the group "connects" with this description, place the slip face up in the middle of your circle or some other visible place. If no one connects with the description, place it face down. Allow time for sharing questions and impressions about the descriptions the group selected.

Digging Deeper 1

Remember Zacchaeus? Read the story about his encounter with Jesus:

Luke 19:1-10

"(Jesus) entered Jericho and was passing through it. A man was there named Zacchaeus; he was a chief tax collector and was rich. He was trying to see who Jesus was, but on account of the crowd he could not, because he was short in stature. So he ran ahead and climbed a sycamore tree to see him, because he was going to pass that way. When Jesus came to the place, he looked up and said to him, 'Zacchaeus, hurry and come down; for I must stay at your house today.' So he hurried down and was happy to welcome him. All who saw it began to grumble and said, 'He has gone to be the guest of one who is a sinner.' Zacchaeus stood there and said to the Lord, 'Look, half of my possessions, Lord, I will give to the poor; and if I have defrauded anyone of anything, I will pay back four times as much.' Then Jesus said to him, 'Today salvation has come to this house, because he too is a son of Abraham. For the Son of Man came to seek out and to save the lost.'"

The list below identifies nine possible outcomes of the experience of salvation in someone's life (and invites you to add to the list). You might call them "signs of salvation." Which one(s) do you see at work in Zacchaeus's experience of salvation? Circle those.

- a heightened awareness of right and wrong
- a desire to learn more about God
- a desire to be more and more like Jesus
- love for all people
- a desire to share God's good news with others
- a desire to know God and spend time with God
- the experience of a new beginning
- a desire for ongoing transformation
- a desire to be with Christians for worship, fellowship, learning, service
- other _____

Think of someone in your congregation you would like to ask "What has salvation meant to you?" Compose a set of questions you could ask this person about their experience of salvation. (Try to find an opportunity to actually interview this person!)

Digging Deeper 2

What is salvation? What is grace? Read the Confession of Faith Summary, looking for handles to help you understand these two "big" words:

Ahead of time, invite someone to class who is willing to be interviewed by your class. (Ask the youth beforehand for a short list of persons whose faith journeys would interest them.) Compose questions as a class to address to your guest. Give the guest a copy of this session beforehand, so he or she knows the context from which the questions will come. Be sure this person understands that the questions will not be available ahead of time.

Write SALVATION in big letters in the middle of a sheet of poster paper. On a second sheet, write GRACE. Have markers available in a variety of colors. Invite youth to record words, phrases, or pictures around these two words that help them understand them.

Confession of Faith Summary

We believe that sin is not the last word, but that God offers all people an alternative to a life that is bound by sin. We believe that through Jesus, God offers us salvation.

We believe that God has offered this alternative since the very beginning—by delivering God's people from slavery in Egypt, and by making a covenant with Israel, for instance. We also believe that Jesus made possible a new covenant for all people. Jesus' coming was an indication of God's great love for the world. Jesus showed us the expanse of this great love by living a life faithful to God's love, even to the point of enduring a painful death on a cross. By his death and resurrection, Jesus breaks the grip of sin and death on the world. Thanks to Jesus, the world knows that love is stronger than sin and life is more powerful than death!

"When we hear the good news of the love of God, the Holy Spirit moves us to accept the gift of salvation." God does not twist our arm to accept this gift. When we do accept it, our response will include yielding to God's grace and turning away from evil. We will repent of sin and put complete trust in God. We will join the fellowship of others who know the gift of salvation. Our words and our actions will reflect the faith that is inside.

We share the news of God's love in our life when we are baptized. In baptism, we publicly acknowledge our salvation and pledge allegiance to God and to the people of God (the church). As we live in the church, we continue growing. We continue to grow in faith and in understanding how to walk faithfully in the way of Christ.

We believe that "we are saved by God's grace, not by our own merits." Our sins are forgiven by grace, not by anything that we do on our own steam. By grace we are healed. By grace we are freed from the bondage of evil. By grace we are delivered from those who do evil against us. No matter how lousy we feel we are, God's grace is big enough to take care of us. No matter how great we feel we are, nothing we can do could possibly be enough to earn salvation. We are saved by God's grace, not by our own merits or lack of them.

We believe that the salvation we already experience is just a taste of the salvation coming in the future. When all of creation experiences salvation in the new heaven and the new earth, the redeemed will live in full communion with God for always.

Respond 1

Return to interview questions you prepared at the end of Digging Deeper 1. Imagine that it is a few years down the road and you are now thirty-five years old. Imagine too that a young person is posing these questions to you. Answer these questions as you hope you could answer them at thirty-five.

This is quite a personal exercise, but if one or two persons are ready to share their replies, let them be interviewed by the class with their own questions.

Respond 2

Have you experienced any of the "signs of salvation" listed in Digging
Deeper 1? Are you experiencing any right now, at this point in your life?
Write a letter to God about how you experienced one of these.

Closing

Record your personal response to this chapter. What has
made an impression on you? What will you remember most?
Was anything exciting? What seems most important? Any
surprises? Do questions remain? Record your personal response in whatever
form you wish: sentences, points, poetry, pictures, music, prayer.

Salvation and Me

9 THE CHURCH OF JESUS CHRIST

Focus

Draw an outline of a body in a page of your scrapbook. Picture your church as this body, with every person playing the role of a different visible body part or vital organ. Which part of the body would you be? Color yourself onto your body outline. Why would you be this particular part?

Explore

Who are the other "parts of the body" in your congregation? Identify at least one person that plays the role of each of these parts. Add to the list if you like. Color these parts onto your body outline.

eye	_____	nose	_____
mouth	_____	ear	_____
arm	_____	hand	_____
leg	_____	foot	_____
neck	_____	heart	_____
lung	_____	stomach	_____
____	_____	____	_____

What observations would you make about this body? Is there anything still missing? Are there clear strengths? Other observations?

As youth arrive, ask for a volunteer to lie down on a piece of newsprint roll. Trace an outline of this person. As each person identifies which part of the body he or she would be, cut that part out of construction paper in a size corresponding to the body outline. Autograph each body part. Glue cut-out body parts onto the body outline. Note: If some parts are overrepresented and others are underrepresented, do not interfere with this.

As other parts are identified, write the people's names on them and add them to your body. Observations?

Digging Deeper 1

Read the Scripture from 1 Corinthians and the Confession of Faith Summary, looking for clues about what makes a healthy body.

1 Corinthians 12:14-27

"Indeed, the body does not consist of one member but of many. If the foot would say, 'Because I am not a hand, I do not belong to the body,' that would not make it any less a part of the body. And if the ear would say, 'Because I am not an eye, I do not belong to the body,' that would not make it any less a part of the body. If the whole body were an eye, where would the hearing be? If the whole body were hearing, where would the sense of smell be? But as it is, God arranged the members in the body, each one of them, as he chose. If all were a single member, where would the body be? As it is, there are many members, yet one body. The eye cannot say to the hand, 'I have no need of you,' nor again the head to the feet, 'I have no need of you.' On the contrary, the members of the body that seem to be weaker are indispensable, and those members of the body that we think less honorable we clothe with greater honor, and our less respectable members are treated with greater respect; whereas our more respectable members do not need this. But God has so arranged the body, giving the greater honor to the inferior member, that there may be no dissension within the body, but the members may have the same care for one another. If one member suffers, all suffer together with it; if one member is honored, all rejoice together with it.

"Now you are the body of Christ and individually members of it."

Confession of Faith Summary

We believe that in the church, all people may come together and find a home. The church embraces persons regardless of nationality, race, class, or gender. Differences that might otherwise divide people can be overcome, thanks to the work of the Holy Spirit. When there are divisions between people or groups, reconciliation and unity may not come easily, but guided by the Spirit's presence and power, this is a possibility.

Whatever the differences are that believers bring to church, there is also much that they have in common. People have chosen to follow Christ in life. They have chosen to be accountable to one another. They have chosen to be accountable to God. These commitments are made, even with the knowledge that the church is imperfect and will make mistakes. But it is also known that the church is aware of its need for repentance when mistakes are made.

Worship is an important part of the life of the church. In worship, the church remembers who it is as God's people of faith. This identity is renewed and strengthened as people worship together. In worship, the church celebrates God's grace and affirms again its loyalty to God. In worship, the church seeks to discern God's will.

The church is the family of God. Like other families, commitment and love are expressed in a number of different ways. When there are physical or spiritual needs, people share with each other. People care for one another, counsel one another, and offer hospitality to all. The church welcomes all who join themselves to Christ to become part of the family of God.

We believe that the church is the body of Christ—that in some mysterious way the church is Jesus Christ in the world. So it is that the church is called to live and minister in the world like Jesus did. Like a human body, the body of Christ has many different members, each with a special gift and function, but all for the common good. Believers are to love each other and to grow toward the likeness of Christ, who is the head of the church.

When we speak of "the church," we refer to people you know as well as many you will never even meet. The church exists as a community of believers in your local congregation, as a community of congregations, as a denomination, and as the worldwide community of faith.

Respond 1

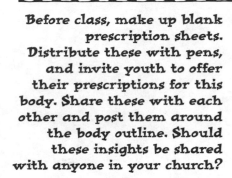

Is your church a healthy body? Imagine that you are a family doctor giving this body its annual physical checkup. As a doctor, you know what a body needs to stay healthy: exercise, rest, nutritious food, appropriate stress, supportive relationships, and perhaps medication. What would you prescribe to this body to make it even healthier? (Keep in mind your own experience of your church and what you have done in this session so far.)

Before class, make up blank prescription sheets. Distribute these with pens, and invite youth to offer their prescriptions for this body. Share these with each other and post them around the body outline. Should these insights be shared with anyone in your church?

Respond 2

How are YOU contributing to the health of this body? How are YOU helping your church to be well-balanced and strong? Are there ways in which your actions actually tear down the body and make it weak? What is your role in relation to your church's health?

Sustain a discussion about your contributions to the health of your church.

Respond 3
(optional)

View the video "Ekklesia: Witnessing to Christ in Today's World," produced in 1992 by Mennonite World Conference and other Mennonite agencies. The video is a window into different ways of being the church around the world. Highly recommended. (Total running time—28 minutes. Study guide included.)

Closing

Record your personal response to this chapter. What has made an impression on you? What will you remember most? Was anything exciting? What seems most important? Any surprises? Do questions remain? Record your personal response in whatever form you wish: sentences, points, poetry, pictures, music, prayer.

The Church and Me

10 THE CHURCH IN MISSION

Focus

Gather these materials before you begin: unsalted popcorn, salt, other popcorn flavorings (ever tried cheese powder or chili powder?), and a sturdy candle.

Light the candle and read this text from Matthew:

Matthew 5:13-16

"'You are the salt of the earth; but if salt has lost its taste, how can its saltiness be restored? It is no longer good for anything, but is thrown out and trampled under foot.

'You are the light of the world. A city built on a hill cannot be hid. No one after lighting a lamp puts it under the bushel basket, but on the lampstand, and it gives light to all in the house. In the same way, let your light shine before others, so that they may see your good works and give glory to your Father in heaven.'"

Before youth arrive, light a sturdy candle in the middle of your meeting area. Around this candle arrange one unlit candle for every member of the group, including yourself. If you are meeting in the evening or if you can darken your meeting room, consider placing a few more candles around and meeting by candlelight. If so, you may need flashlights on hand for Digging Deeper 1. Begin by reading the text from Matthew.

Explore

Taste the unsalted popcorn. Then try the popcorn with salt and other flavorings. While you are munching, ponder this: If "mission" means "living out the love that God has entrusted us with," then what does this text from Matthew have to do with mission?

Munch on unsalted popcorn, then popcorn you have prepared with different flavors. (As a second choice, substitute different flavors of potato chips for the popcorn. Include unsalted potato chips or pretzels.) Ponder the question about mission.

Digging Deeper 1

Read the Confession of Faith Summary, looking for different ways that the church lives out its mission.

Invite youth to underline or highlight different aspects of mission as they read. When ready, call out these different mission activities. Pick up on anything that is not understood.

Confession of Faith Summary

We believe that when Jesus commissioned the disciples to continue his ministry, he was also commissioning us and others who followed. We continue Jesus' ministry of gathering the new people of God. Like the disciples, we receive the Holy Spirit to carry out Jesus' mission of preaching, teaching, healing, and announcing the kingdom of God.

For the church, an important part of announcing the kingdom of God is putting into practise what Jesus lived and taught. The church seeks to show "the world a sample of life under the lordship of Christ." Life under the lordship of Christ will look different than society's way of life. So the church is like a city on a hill—a light to the nations.

The church is called to witness to the reign of Christ in both word and deed. "The church is to seek the lost, call for repentance, announce salvation from sin, proclaim the gospel of peace, set free the oppressed, pray for righteousness and justice, serve as Jesus did, and without coercion urge all people to become part of the people of God. The church is called to be a channel of God's healing." Followers filled with the love of Christ will be compelled to witness for their Savior even at the risk of suffering and death.

When new believers acknowledge Christ as Lord and Savior, they are welcomed into the church. New Christians learn to participate in all aspects of the church's life: worship, fellowship, education, mutual aid, decision making, service, and continuing mission. New believers have much to offer the church. They offer new perspectives and "help the church to learn new dimensions of its mission."

The church may be thought of as "God's nation," welcoming people from every country and ethnic background. In the same vein, God calls the church to extend its mission to people from every race and nationality. The church's mission is to create one new humanity, reconciling groups with deeply felt differences. The church's hope is to provide a "preview of that day when all the nations shall stream to the mountain of the Lord and be at peace."

Digging Deeper 2

Our denomination has embraced a statement that identifies our priorities for mission, called "Vision: Healing and Hope." Read this statement. See if you can memorize it in five minutes.

Vision: Healing and Hope

"God calls us to be followers of Jesus Christ and,
by the power of the Holy Spirit,
to grow as communities of grace, joy and peace,
so that God's healing and hope flow through us to the world."

Offer five minutes for youth to memorize the statement. If your mood is lively, see how long it would take the whole group to memorize it. Help each other. Once people have it in their heads, they can help others.

Respond 1

Having a vision statement is like having a new pair of glasses and a good quality telescope. The new glasses help you see what is around you more clearly. The telescope helps you look beyond where you are and gaze at new possibilities. First, put on the new glasses and identify ways that your congregation shows it is a community of grace, joy, and peace. How is your congregation offering healing and hope to the world? Second, look through the telescope and identify ways your congregation could grow in these areas. Record your ideas in the chart below. Fill in the blank with the name of your congregation.

Living as a community of grace, joy, and peace at _____, so that God's healing and hope flow through us to the world

What Is   **What Can Be**

Divide the class into two groups. Ask one group to focus on "what is," and the other to focus on "what can be." Report back and add to each other's list. Are there leaders in the congregation with whom these insights should be shared?

Respond 2

You have thought about your congregation, now what about yourself? How can you be an agent of healing and hope in your setting?

Share your ideas with each other.

Respond 3

Copy the Vision: Healing and Hope logo and make something to wear or display. One idea is to copy the logo on an overhead transparency. Add color if you like. Cut it out and stick it on your bedroom window.

Order Vision: Healing and Hope bookmarks from your denominational office. Distribute at the end of class. If you use the overhead transparency idea, the logos do not need to be any larger than the logo on the bookmark. You should be able to get twelve on one transparency.

Darken the room if it is not dark already. Light the "Christ candle" if it is not still lit from the beginning of class. Distribute the remaining candles, and pass the light from the Christ candle to each other. Watch the room brighten. For a closing prayer, sing or read "You are salt for the earth" (Hymnal: A Worship Book, #226).

Closing

Record your personal response to this chapter. What has made an impression on you? What will you remember most? Was anything exciting? What seems most important? Any surprises? Do questions remain? Record your personal response in whatever form you wish: sentences, points, poetry, pictures, music, prayer.

Mission and Me

11 BAPTISM

Focus

Recall a baptism you have observed. What do you remember about this baptism? Are you left with certain feelings or impressions? Did it raise any questions for you?

Explore

Explore some of your impressions about baptism. Mark each of the following statements true or false. What do you think?

____ Baptism is the beginning of the Christian journey.

____ Mennonites believe you must be eighteen to be baptized.

____ A good reason to be baptized is to please your parents.

____ You can be a member of the church without being baptized.

____ It matters how you are baptized (sprinkle, pour, immersion).

____ Persons who were baptized as infants must be rebaptized as adults.

____ It is possible to be baptized without becoming a member of a congregation.

____ If you feel like it, you can be baptized again later.

____ Baptism comes only after a dramatic conversion experience.

____ Baptism is the end of the Christian journey.

Digging Deeper 1

Read the Confession of Faith Summary with this question in mind: "Should I wait to be baptized until I have my faith all figured out?" How does this article respond to this question and others you bring to it?

Before you meet, gather whatever vessels your congregation uses for a baptism (i.e., pitcher, towel, basin, etc.). Arrange these things someplace in your meeting room where they are visible to the group. If your congregation baptises by immersion, consider having this session at the baptistry or body of water commonly used for baptism. If questions arise, simply note these for now and return to them in the Digging Deeper 2 exercise.

Share your ideas by forming a human continuum: designate one end of the room "true" and the other "false." For each statement, place yourself where you want to be on the continuum. With the exception of questions of clarity, hold other questions or discussion until later (see Digging Deeper 2).

Confession of Faith Summary

We believe that God's Holy Spirit moves among us even today and that baptism is a sign of the continuing work of the Spirit in the lives of believers. Through the Spirit, we have the courage to turn around—to repent and turn toward God in faith. Because we are baptized in the Spirit, we can offer Christ's healing to others, live in community, and do ever so many other things that are part of this life.

We believe that when someone is baptized, something very important is happening during that moment, has happened already, and will happen in the future. What has happened? The person has repented and received forgiveness; the person has encountered the grace of God in Christ Jesus. What is happening? The person is being incorporated into Christ's body on earth—the church. What will happen? The person looks forward to a life empowered by the Spirit to live out the pledges made at baptism: to serve Christ and to minister as a member of his body, according to the gifts given to each one.

If the baptism of water is a sign that we have repented and is made possible by the baptism of the Spirit, it is also a public commitment to identify with Jesus. Jesus understood the giving of his life for others as a baptism—the baptism of blood. When we commit ourselves to identify with Jesus, we are saying that we are open to following Jesus' example of loving enemies and renouncing violence, even if this means we may need to suffer for it.

"Christian baptism is for those who confess their sins, repent, accept Jesus Christ as Savior and Lord, and commit themselves to follow Christ in obedience as members of his body, both giving and receiving care and counsel in the church. Baptism is for those who are of the age of accountability and who freely request baptism on the basis of their response to Jesus Christ in faith."

Digging Deeper 2

Return to the True/False exercise in Explore. Many Mennonites would likely answer false to these statements (although there may be special circumstances that could differ from this). Look back over your responses and note any questions that remain for you.

Who could explore these questions with you: a parent, pastor, Sunday school teacher, sponsor, mentor?

Return to the True/False exercise, and pick up questions raised. In preparation, you may wish to read the material on baptism in _Confession of Faith in a Mennonite Perspective_, pp. 46-49. Does your congregation have particular traditions for baptisms that would be good to identify and explore?

Digging Deeper 3

According to Galatians 3, when we are baptized, we become "one in Christ" with others in the church. Barriers that might arise between people in other settings melt away between children of God. Read Galatians 3:26-29 with a eye out for three examples of barriers between people that baptism in Christ breaks down. Highlight or underline these examples.

Galatians 3:26-29

"... for in Christ Jesus you are all children of God through faith. As many of you as were baptized into Christ have clothed yourselves with Christ. There is no longer Jew or Greek, there is no longer slave or free, there is no longer male and female; for all of you are one in Christ Jesus. And if you belong to Christ, then you are Abraham's offspring, heirs according to the promise."

What does it mean to be "one in Christ?" How does your congregation reflect this?

Pinpoint one place where you see the reality of being "one in Christ."

Is there another place where it could happen even more?

Unless your group is very small, encourage youth to work in twos or threes. Share the responses from the questions that follow reading the text with the whole group. Are there leaders in the church who could benefit from hearing youths' perspectives on these questions? How might that happen?

Respond 1

If you would be baptized, what gifts of ministry could you contribute to the church and to the work of God in the world? What would you like to offer?

Be prepared to talk about the different ministries of your congregation and how the gifts and skills of youth in your group could strengthen these ministries.

Respond 2

On the other hand, what would you hope to receive from God or from the church? What could be offered to you?

As youth ponder this question, you may wish to encourage them to imagine stages of life beyond teenage and young adulthood.

Respond 3

Have your parents been baptized? Ask them to tell you their baptism story. Does their story influence you in any way? If so, how?

Invite someone from the congregation to class to share their baptism story. Encourage youth to talk with their parents about their baptism story.

While this may seem an obvious question, it should not be assumed. Make certain that each youth has an option that feels comfortable to them. If you are planning to connect with each youth individually at some point in the course of your meetings, explain to them what you are planning and when it might happen.

Closing prayer: Kneel and recite the Lord's Prayer together.

Respond 4

If you felt led to explore baptism, how would you follow through on this? Who would you talk to?

Closing

Record your personal response to this chapter. What has made an impression on you? What will you remember most? Was anything exciting? What seems most important? Any surprises? Do questions remain? Record your personal response in whatever form you wish: sentences, points, poetry, pictures, music, prayer.

Baptism and Me

12 THE LORD'S SUPPER

Focus

Find yourself some "real" bread, and thick grape juice. Spend some time with it: feel it; smell it; taste it. Reflect on how nourishing food keeps our bodies healthy and growing. Reflect too on how faith keeps our spirits healthy and growing.

Explore 1

What are your experiences with communion? From the following list, check all the feelings that apply to you and your experience of the Lord's Supper so far:

_____ a sense of awe about what was happening

_____ puzzled by what it all means

_____ resentment at not being fully included

_____ eagerness for a time when I will take communion too

_____ to be honest, a little bored

_____ other:

Explore 2

When we participate in the Lord's Supper, we are reenacting the Last Supper that Jesus shared with the disciples. They gathered in an out-of-the-way room to share the Passover meal together. Jesus "took a loaf of bread, and when he had given thanks, he broke it and gave it to them, saying, 'This is my body, which is given for you. Do this in remembrance of me.' And he did the same with the cup after supper, saying, 'This cup that is poured out for you is the new covenant in my blood'" (Luke 22:19-20).

If you were one of the disciples present at this meal, what might you be thinking?

Distribute hunks of homemade bread and glasses of grape juice. Simply enjoy them, and continue sharing feelings and memories associated with communion.

After completing this list, share with each other the range of feelings associated with the Lord's Supper.

Create a quiet mood for imagining this scene. Use candlelight, as this supper originally happened long before electric lighting! Play some worshipful music, if you like.

What might you be feeling?

How would you respond when Jesus hands you the bread?

What do you think Jesus meant when he said, "This is my body, which is given for you"?

What would you say to Jesus in reply?

What would Jesus say back to you?

Digging Deeper 1

What are we doing when we celebrate the Lord's Supper? One important dimension is that we are remembering Jesus, but that is not the only possibility. Read the text from 1 Corinthians and the Confession of Faith Summary. Note in the margins other responses to the question "What are we doing when we celebrate the Lord's Supper?"

1 Corinthians 11:23-26

"For I received from the Lord what I also handed on to you, that the Lord Jesus on the night when he was betrayed took a loaf of bread, and when he had given thanks, he broke it and said, 'This is my body that is for you. Do this in remembrance of me.' In the same way he took the cup also, after supper, saying, 'This cup is the new covenant in my blood. Do this, as often as you drink it, in remembrance of me.' For as often as you eat this bread and drink the cup, you proclaim the Lord's death until he comes."

Confession of Faith Summary

The Lord's Supper (or "communion," as it is sometimes called) helps us remember Jesus. As we eat the bread and drink the cup together, we ponder the sacrifices and suffering that Jesus lived through to show the world what God's love is like and to give us a new connection with God. We celebrate that death did not have the last word: God raised Jesus from the dead! Jesus' resurrection leads us to thank God for this and other awesome things God has done and continues to do.

We believe that the risen Christ still lives and is present in the church. Touching the bread and tasting the cup is a sign that Christ is just as present as these elements. We are also reminded that food and drink are not the only things we need to sustain our lives—Christ also sustains us.

The Lord's Supper also helps believers recommit themselves to follow Jesus in God's way. Believers may return with new energy to the promises they made to God when they were baptized. They may think again about their need to confess their sins, or their desire to give and receive forgiveness. Sharing the bread and the cup renews our bond to God, to each other, and to all believers throughout the world and throughout history.

The Lord's table is a welcoming table. "All are invited to the Lord's table who have been baptized into the community of faith, are living at peace with God and with their brothers and sisters in the faith, and are willing to be accountable in their congregation."

The Lord's Supper does not just look back; it also looks forward. Some day, the reign of God will come completely. Good will finally win out over evil, just as life won out over death when God raised Jesus. When believers share the bread and cup, they celebrate in joy! They celebrate in hope!

Respond 1

The Confession of Faith ties the Lord's Supper and baptism together. It claims that a key part of communion is remembering the promises you made to God when you were baptized, and thinking again about what that means for your life. With this understanding, it doesn't make sense to participate in communion before you are baptized. It would be like celebrating your anniversary before you got married!

Think through the issue about who participates in communion from the two angles outlined below. Try to think broadly—you need not agree with what you write! (If this issue is important to you, identify someone in the church with whom you could talk about your concerns.)

better wait ...

What are some good reasons for waiting to participate in the Lord's Supper until you are baptized? Using the material above and your own reflections, jot down what some good reasons might be.

open invitation ...

Do you think there are times when anyone who wants to should be invited to take communion? What are your reasons for this perspective?

Divide the class into two groups, assigning one of these perspectives to each group. Stage a debate between the two groups on this issue.

Respond 2

Can you hear Jesus' invitation to eat this bread and drink this cup with him? How will you respond?

Closing prayer: Darken the room and light one of the candles you used during Explore 2. Take turns holding the candle. Gather around the person with the candle, lay hands on this person, and voice prayers of thanksgiving for him or her.

Closing

Record your personal response to this chapter. What has made an impression on you? What will you remember most? Was anything exciting? What seems most important? Any surprises? Do questions remain? Record your personal response in whatever form you wish: sentences, points, poetry, pictures, music, prayer.

The Lord's Supper and Me

13 FOOT WASHING

Focus

When it comes to servanthood, where do you draw the line? What would you be happy to do in service for another person? What might you be willing to do? Is there anything you would not do? Look at the list below and decide where you would be on the "servanthood scale." (Check where you would be on the continuum.)

clean toilets at church	sure • • • ● ● • •	no way
change the diaper of a baby	sure • • • ● ● • •	no way
wash someone's hair	sure • • ● ● ● • •	no way
pick up other people's litter	sure • • ● ● ● • •	no way
change the diaper of a senior	sure • • ● ● ● • •	no way
wash windows for a grandparent	sure • • ● ● ● • •	no way
babysit without pay	sure • • ● ● ● • •	no way
give up your seat on the bus to a senior	sure • • ● ● ● • •	no way
give up your place in a line for a mom with a baby	sure • • ● ● ● • •	no way
take your little brother or sister along with you and your friends	sure • • ● ● ● • •	no way
wash someone's feet	sure • ● ● ● ● • •	no way

Look back at your responses. Did you learn anything about your attitudes to servanthood?

Is servanthood more than doing menial tasks for others? If so, what is it?

Explore

Read the excerpt from John 13. In Jesus' day, people's feet got tired and dirty on the hot, dusty roads. Feet were often washed by the household servants, but never by the master of

In a group setting, identify one end of the room as "sure" and the other as "no way." Read the tasks below one at a time. Ask youth to stand at the place on the continuum that indicates where they are.

Act out the excerpt from John 13 with five people. You will need three speakers (Narrator, Jesus, Peter) and two actors to mime what is spoken (Jesus and Peter). You may wish to use these props: large towel, basin, and water.

the house. Try to imagine how Simon Peter would have felt in this situation.

John 13:3-9; 14-15

"Jesus, knowing that the Father had given all things into his hands, and that he had come from God and was going to God, got up from the table, took off his outer robe, and tied a towel around himself. Then he poured water into a basin and began to wash the disciples' feet and to wipe them with the towel that was tied around him. He came to Simon Peter, who said to him, 'Lord, are you going to wash my feet?' Jesus answered, 'You do not know now what I am doing, but later you will understand.' Peter said to him, 'You will never wash my feet.' Jesus answered, 'Unless I wash you, you have no share with me.' Simon Peter said to him, 'Lord, not my feet only but also my hands and my head!'. . . (Jesus said), 'So if I, your Lord and Teacher, have washed your feet, you also ought to wash one another's feet. For I have set you an example, that you also should do as I have done to you.'"

Digging Deeper 1

Read the article paraphrase from the Confession of Faith. What is Jesus' attitude to servanthood? What is the church's attitude to servanthood? Highlight or underline relevant points—in different colors if you like.

Confession of Faith Summary

We believe that Jesus Christ calls us to serve one another in love just like he did. Jesus showed us one example of serving another in love just before his death. On this occasion, Jesus stooped to wash the disciples' feet, demonstrating humility and servanthood. He also showed us humility and servanthood when he laid down his life on the cross. So in washing the disciples' feet, Jesus was modeling an attitude or approach to life that he would soon take to an extreme. Jesus also invites his disciples to follow in his footsteps of humble service.

Sometimes congregations include foot washing in their worship, often linked with communion. When believers wash each others' feet, they show that they are aware of their need of cleansing. They show that they are willing to let go of pride and worldly power. They also show their willingness to offer their lives in humble service and sacrificial love. When believers wash each others' feet, they share in the body of Christ.

Respond 1
(if your congregation practises foot washing)

Have you ever observed or participated in a foot washing service? Was it a meaningful experience for you? Why?

Chat with an adult in your congregation about what foot washing means to them.

Arrange for a guest to join you to respond to the question "What does foot washing mean to you?" This could be an older person who may remember various ways the congregation has practised foot washing.

Respond 2
(if your congregation does not practise foot washing)

Why doesn't your congregation practise foot washing? Are there other expressions of servanthood that your congregation practises?

Be sure you are familiar with your congregation's history on foot washing. Also be familiar with the material on foot washing in <u>Confession of Faith in a Mennonite Perspective</u>, pp. 53-54.

Respond 3
(for a group)

Chat with your pastor or youth leader about finding a setting for an experience of hand washing. Begin by reading the text above from John 13, or #783 in *Hymnal: A Worship Book*. Pass a towel and basin around the circle, each person washing and drying the hands of the next and saying, "My friend, may you know the peace and the power of Christ's love." Close by singing "Will you let me be your servant," *Hymnal: A Worship Book*, #307.

Close the session with hand washing—or foot washing, if that seems more appropriate.

Closing

Record your personal response to this chapter. What has made an impression on you? What will you remember most? Was anything exciting? What seems most important? Any surprises? Do questions remain? Record your personal response in whatever form you wish: sentences, points, poetry, pictures, music, prayer.

Foot Washing and Me

Closing prayer: Darken the room and light a candle. Speak these words as you pass the candle from one person to the next: "My friend, may you know the peace and the power of Christ's love." Close with a prayer of thanksgiving for Jesus' example of servanthood.

14 DISCIPLINE IN THE CHURCH

Focus

Two longtime friends have had a falling out. Hurts run deep. They take to gossiping and spreading lies about each other. There is a lot of pain. One of the friends approaches their youth leader saying, "I feel really bad that we're not on speaking terms. What can I do about this?" When you read this anecdote, what do you feel inside?

Choose two people to play the role of the two friends. Have them invent what their issues are and how terribly the other person has treated them. Others in the group can help them create a messy but realistic scenario.

Explore

Step into the shoes of the youth leader of the two friends described above. What options could you propose to the one who approached you?

Digging Deeper 1

What ideas did Jesus have about handling conflicts between people? Read his teaching in Matthew 18:

Role-play Jesus' instructions about confronting in love: starting with one and proceeding to larger numbers if necessary.

Matthew 18:15-20

"'If another member of the church sins against you, go and point out the fault when the two of you are alone. If the member listens to you, you have regained that one. But if you are not listened to, take one or two others along with you, so that every word may be confirmed by the evidence of two or three witnesses. If the member refuses to listen to them, tell it to the church; and if the offender refuses to listen even to the church, let such a one be to you as a Gentile and a tax collector. Truly I tell you, whatever you bind on earth will be bound in heaven, and whatever you loose on earth will be loosed in heaven. Again, truly I tell you, if two of you agree on earth about anything you ask, it will be done for you by my Father in heaven. For where two or three are gathered in my name, I am there among them.'"

Digging Deeper 2

Suppose there was a conflict in your church and doing what is described in Matthew 18 did not resolve the problem. How would the church proceed? Read the Confession of Faith Summary, looking for ideas.

Confession of Faith Summary

We believe that the practice of discipline in the church is part of the good news. According to Jesus and the apostles, all believers seek to be open to the church's mutual care and discipline. Jesus gave the church authority to discern right from wrong. Therefore, believers commit themselves to give and receive counsel within the faith community on important matters.

If a brother or sister errs, discipline should be offered in a spirit of encouragement and caring: "speaking the truth in love." Normally, discipline will lead to "confession, forgiveness, and reconciliation." What does discipline look like? First, there is direct conversation between the erring person and another member. "Depending on the person's response, admonition may continue within a broader circle. This usually includes a pastor or congregational leader. If necessary, the matter may finally be brought to the congregation. A brother or sister who repents is to be forgiven and encouraged in making the needed change.

"If the erring member persists in sin without repentance and rejects even the admonition of the congregation, membership may be suspended. Suspension of membership is the recognition that persons have separated themselves from the body of Christ. When this occurs, the church continues to pray for them and seeks to restore them to its fellowship."

We believe that when discipline is correctly understood and practiced with compassion, it enhances the church's witness because it helps maintain the church's integrity. Spirit-led discipline can lead the way to forgiveness and new life in Christ.

Respond 1

Distribute these different roles and perspectives among the people in your group. Have them tell the rest of the group what their feelings are.

Try to imagine what a process like the one described here would feel like from a number of different perspectives. Try to identify three feelings that each of the following people might experience in the middle of an exercise of discipline (i.e., you don't know yet how it's all going to turn out):

erring member _____

friends of the erring member _____

the pastor _____

congregational leaders _____

other members of the congregation _____

children in the congregation _____

Respond 2

If or when your congregation embarks on a process of discipline, what are some important things you think should be remembered by everyone involved? Put your ideas into people's mouths! We need each other to help us remember important things:

On newsprint or chalkboard, draw a number of empty blurps. Invite youth to add their own faces and comments.

Closing

Record your personal response to this chapter. What has made an impression on you? What will you remember most? Was anything exciting? What seems most important? Any surprises? Do questions remain? Record your personal response in whatever form you wish: sentences, points, poetry, pictures, music, prayer.

Discipline and Me

Closing prayer: Pray together #765 in Hymnal: A Worship Book, or some other prayer that celebrates God's patience, compassion, and love.

15 MINISTRY AND LEADERSHIP

Focus

When you think about leaders in the church, who comes to mind? The church has leaders in many different roles. Some of them you may know, some you may not. Try to identify at least one person who serves in each of the leadership roles listed below. Not all of this list may apply to your setting. (For instance, some churches have elders while others have deacons.)

pastor _____

deacon _____

elder _____

evangelist _____

missionary _____

teacher (in the church) _____

conference minister _____

overseer _____

mentor _____

Are there others in your church who you look to as leaders but do not fit into these categories? Add them to your list. List their title or what they do on the left, and put their names on the right:

_____ _____

_____ _____

_____ _____

_____ _____

> If you have four or more people, divide your group in half, set a timer for two minutes, and see which group can come up with the most complete list in the given time. If your group is too small for this, race against the clock.

Explore

When it comes to leadership, three important words in the language of the church are **call**, **discernment**, and **accountability**. Each of these stories illustrates one of these words. Try to identify which word goes with each story. (Check your matches in Appendix 1 when you are done.)

_____ "I wasn't sure if I should agree to help the worship committee of our church plan the Easter service. They asked me to, but I didn't know if I could do it, even though it sounded exciting. I decided to ask some other people what they thought. I talked to my Sunday school teacher, my parents, and a friend. They all thought I could do it. In fact, my Sunday school teacher thought I had something important to offer. I thought about it and prayed about it too. I decided to say yes."

_____ "I was having fun with some of my friends teasing somebody in our youth group. Actually, "dissecting" would be more like it. I realize now I was pretty cruel, but my friends thought I was hilarious. We hadn't noticed that one of our youth sponsors was in the kitchen and could hear us. Later in the evening, she approached me about it when we were alone. She asked me the obvious questions, like how would I feel if someone said those things about me? At the time, I was embarrassed and a little angry, but later I was glad she spoke to me. I don't want to be the kind of person that tears others down. I needed that reminder."

_____ "I had planned to work at the ice cream shop this summer, but lately I keep thinking about helping out at our church's summer camp. I wouldn't make as much money, but that wouldn't be the end of the world. I enjoyed learning about the camp at our youth retreat, and talking with one of last year's counselors. I just can't shake the idea. It keeps coming back—even when I'm not praying."

Have you ever experienced call, discernment, or accountability? What was that experience?

 # Digging Deeper 1

Read the text from Ephesians, and the Confession of Faith Summary. Who is called to ministry? Are only certain people "qualified" for ministry? What do you find here?

Ephesians 4:11-16

"The gifts he gave were that some would be apostles, some prophets, some evangelists, some pastors and teachers, to equip the saints for the work of ministry, for building up the body of Christ, until all of us come to the unity of the faith and of the knowledge of the Son of God, to maturity, to the measure of the full stature of Christ. We must no longer be children, tossed to and fro and blown about by every wind of doctrine, by people's trickery, by their craftiness in deceitful scheming. But speaking the truth in love, we must grow up in every way into him who is the head, into Christ, from whom the whole body, joined and knit together by every ligament with which it is equipped, as each part is working properly, promotes the body's growth in building itself up in love."

Confession of Faith Summary

We believe that Christ invites all Christians to minister to each other and to people beyond the church. This does not mean that all Christians will be pastors or missionaries. It does mean that each of us has something to offer the church. Christ will help us respond to needs that we see; Christ will enable us to answer to opportunities to lead and serve. When we respond to this call, we help build up the body of Christ and become part of God's creative work.

The church calls gifted men and women to lead and serve on its behalf. Leaders such as teachers, pastors, missionaries, deacons, elders, and others may be called by the church, trained by the church, and appointed by the church to do their work. Part of the task of these leaders is to lead the congregation in faithful living so that the church may be "built together spiritually into a dwelling place for God" (Ephesians 2:22) .

Sometimes, after a person has prepared to lead and has been tested and accepted, there is a service to celebrate! This may be a service of ordination or some other act. In this celebration, the church indicates its blessing and support. The new leader is reminded of his or her responsibility to God and the church. Everyone is reminded of the need to encourage each other in ministry.

Digging Deeper 2

The Scriptures give us insights into different aspects of faithful leadership within the church. Look up these Scriptures and note what aspect of ministry each talks about. (Check your answers against the key in Appendix 1.)

2 Timothy 4:1-3   _____

Matthew 9:35-37   _____

1 Timothy 4:13   _____

Philippians 2:1-4   _____

Titus 2:15   _____

Ephesians 4:11-13   _____

For a lively touch, divide into two groups. Give the biblical references out one at a time, and see which team can come up with the answer first. A bell for each team to ring when they get an answer would enhance the fun.

Respond 1

Identify a leader in your church you would like to interview. Look back over the material in this chapter and prepare a list of questions to ask this person. Make notes from your interview and keep them in your scrapbook.

Ahead of time, invite a leader in your congregation (i.e., an elder or deacon) to join your class at this point. Interview this person from the questions identified during this exercise.

In a group setting, spotlight one person at a time, starting with "Rachel." Hand out slips of paper, and invite everyone to write Rachel's name at the top, and below it, one gift that they recognize in Rachel. Use this list for ideas, but do not be limited by it. Once everyone has been spotlighted, put the slips in piles with all the slips relating to Rachel on one pile, etc. Distribute the piles so that no one has their own pile. Conclude with the "Closing prayer."

Respond 2

What are your gifts for ministry? How do you help build up the body of Christ? How are you part of God's creative work? Check everything from the list below that applies to you. Give the list a custom fit by adding to it gifts that might be unique to you. Don't be shy!

_____ I can make things with my hands.

_____ I like being in dramas.

_____ I can encourage people when they are down.

_____ I can help people get organized.

_____ I can care for children.

_____ I can speak in public.

_____ I like to visit with elderly people.

_____ I have a musical gift that I can share in worship or other settings.

_____ When there's a job to be done, I pitch right in.

_____ I have a lot of compassion to share when people have problems.

_____ I can help others study the Bible.

_____ I can pray.

_____ I can speak out with courage when I recognize injustice.

_____ I can make banners.

_____ I can help with our Bible School or other children's programs.

_____ _____

_____ _____

Closing prayer: In prayer, thank God for each person by name, and read off the gifts identified for that person in Respond 2. For each person, respond with the refrain "Thank-you for _____ and his/her gifts for ministry."

Closing

Record your personal response to this chapter. What has made an impression on you? What will you remember most? Was anything exciting? What seems most important? Any surprises? Do questions remain? Record your personal response in whatever form you wish: sentences, points, poetry, pictures, music, prayer.

Ministry and Me

16 CHURCH ORDER AND UNITY

Focus

Have you heard the fable from India about the elephant and the blind men? Each one felt a different part of the elephant and described what they thought an elephant looked like according to the part that each felt. The one that felt the elephant's leg thought an elephant was like a tree trunk. The one who felt its tail thought an elephant was like a rope, etc. Their ideas weren't wrong, they just weren't complete. Not until they all got together did a more accurate picture of an elephant come together.

If the blind men visited your home and encountered your bicycle, iron, or refrigerator, what would they "see"? Choose one of these objects and note how it might be described by these men, each feeling a different part.

Explore

Take a tour of your church's sanctuary or meeting area. Walk around and sit in places where you don't usually sit. Include on your tour places that you don't visit very often: the pulpit area, nursery, sound booth, organ or piano bench, etc. While you are touring, ask yourself how your worship service would be experienced differently from each of these different perspectives.

What did you learn from your tour?

Are there other areas of church life (besides your worship service) that might be experienced from a number of different perspectives? What are some areas that come to mind?

Place a small table in the middle of your meeting area. On the table, place a large cardboard box on which you have written a different descriptive message or picture about the box on each side, including the top. Place another descriptive message or picture underneath the table so it may be viewed by someone lying on the floor. Cover the box with a sheet until you are ready for the exercise. Position youth around the room so that they will look at the box from different perspectives, including lying on the floor and being elevated by a desk or ladder. Remove the sheet. Share your perspectives with each other to build an accurate description of the box. Which perspective is most important? Any unnecessary perspectives? Any points of overlap or outright differences?

Digging Deeper 1

Read the text from Ephesians and the Confession of Faith Summary, looking for ideas about how a church becomes strong with the help of different perspectives. How does a church bring different perspectives together into unity?

Ephesians 2:19-22

"So then you are no longer strangers and aliens, but you are citizens with the saints and also members of the household of God, built upon the foundation of the apostles and prophets, with Christ Jesus himself as the cornerstone. In him the whole structure is joined together and grows into a holy temple in the Lord; in whom you also are built together spiritually into a dwelling place for God."

Confession of Faith Summary

When a house is built, many different kinds of materials are used. There are beams and joists to provide a structure, mortar to hold the bricks together, windows to let in light and fresh air, and shingles to protect from rain. Every part of the house has a contribution to make to the whole. When all come together, you have a picture of order and unity. So it is with the church. Like a house, a congregation is strong because of its many different parts. When these parts work together in unity, they build up the body of Christ. A brick flying through the air can do a lot of damage to a window. But a brick in place beside a window contributes to the strength and beauty of the structure. When the members of a church can reach across their differences to serve and be served, the body of Christ is built up in love and is a witness to the world of God's love.

In the life of a church, many decisions must be made. Members of the church listen and speak in a spirit of prayerful openness. They know that sometimes their point of view will be affirmed and sometimes it will be corrected. The Scriptures are the constant guide in this process of discernment. Sometimes decisions take a long time to make. "It is better to wait patiently for a word from the Lord leading toward consensus than to make hasty decisions."

Just as different members come together to build up the congregation, different congregations come together to build up the wider church in larger assemblies and conferences. Local congregations seek the counsel of the wider church in important matters. Once again, sometimes their point of view will be affirmed and sometimes it will be corrected. Churches hold each other accountable to Christ and to one another on all levels of church life.

Respond 1

What does a congregation "look like" when it is living in unity? How will people relate to each other? How might decisions be made? Work through the list below, indicating whether you think each item should always happen (A), sometimes happen (S), or never happen (N). (When you are finished, compare your responses with those in Appendix 1.)

In order to build unity in a church ...

A S N people will treat each other with respect

A S N people will pray for each other and with each other

A S N people will disagree

A S N it is good to tell someone how you feel about something

A S N people will be angry with each other

A S N if the Holy Spirit is part of making a decision, it will happen quickly

A S N someone may express their love for me by disagreeing with me or challenging me

A S N you should keep your opinions to yourself

A S N people will talk about others behind their backs

A S N every person should have a strongly held opinion on every issue

Identify three places in the room to correspond with "always," "sometimes," and "never." For each item, ask youth to move to the place that matches their answer. Ask why a certain response was chosen, or why another response was not chosen.

Respond 2

(for a group)

Imagine this situation:

Some youth in your congregation have decided to attend the youth convention being held next summer. To assist with travel and registration costs, these youth decide to have some fund-raisers. The first fund-raiser will be a raffle. Three prizes have been arranged, all donated by the families of the youth who hope to go to the convention: a rose bush, the church's history book that is now out of print and hard to find, and a gourmet meal for six. The youth printed up the raffle tickets and started selling them on Sunday morning. Some people bought the tickets enthusiastically. Others were offended by the notion of a raffle. Some thought that the youth shouldn't be selling the tickets on Sunday morning. A meeting has been called to discuss the issue of the youth using a raffle as a fund-raiser.

The people listed below come to the meeting. The feelings of each are indicated as well as the reason behind that feeling. Role play a meeting where people with these different perspectives try to work toward unity on this issue:

• a youth hoping to go to the convention (feeling hurt, because the church is not supporting their idea)

Write each of these roles on a slip of paper, place them in a basket, and distribute them to the youth. If you have a large group, assign multiple people to some roles. If you have a small group, leave some of the roles out.

- a youth who can't go to the convention (feeling resentful, because some youth who can't go to the convention feel too much energy is going into fund-raisers)
- a parent who donated one of the prizes (feeling irritated, because a lot of effort had gone into organizing the raffle already)
- a youth sponsor (feeling embarrassed, because he/she did not anticipate this issue)
- the church council chairperson (feeling angry, because he/she views raffles as a form of gambling)
- an elder or deacon (feeling sad, because he/she views selling anything at church on Sunday morning an inappropriate use of God's house, and feels the youth should have known this)

At the end of the role play, return the slips of paper to the basket to symbolize that the roles are being put away. Ask each other the following questions:

How did you feel in your role?
What did you observe about yourself or others?
What did you learn?
Was it easy to work at building unity?
How did you do in comparison to the guidelines listed in Respond 1?

Respond 3
(optional)

Of what group of congregations is your church a part? Visit the offices of your conference or district, or invite a staff member to visit you. Talk with the staff to learn about their work, their vision for the church, and the challenges they face. Work at understanding how your congregation fits into a larger network of congregations.

 # Closing

Record your personal response to this chapter. What has made an impression on you? What will you remember most? Was anything exciting? What seems most important? Any surprises? Do questions remain? Record your personal response in whatever form you wish: sentences, points, poetry, pictures, music, prayer.

Church Order and Unity and Me

Closing prayer: Distribute strips of paper of different colors (about 1.5" by 8.5"). Invite youth to write prayers for unity on as many strips as they wish. Tape the ends of the strips while linking them together to form a paper chain. Each time a new link of the chain is added, voice this refrain: "In Christ, everyone is joined together." Hang the chain somewhere in your meeting area.

17
DISCIPLESHIP AND THE CHRISTIAN LIFE

Focus

Imagine the following scene. You are driving a car, alone, on a country road. You are on your way to a much-longed-for job interview. Looking ahead, you see that a car has slid off the road into the ditch. As you get closer, you see the driver slumped over the steering wheel. You start to brake, then you glance at your watch. If you stop, you will miss your interview. What do you do?

Read this dilemma aloud. Give everyone a chance to think about what their response would be. Share with each other what you would do.

Explore

In the face of this dilemma, why did you make the choice you did? On what basis did you make this decision? What forms the foundation for this and other tough decisions you need to make?

Carry forward the discussion in Focus, perhaps without a noticeable break. Explore what forms the base from which hard decisions are made. If the details of the situation were changed (for example, if the driver was not injured), would it make a difference?

Digging Deeper 1

When faced with tough decisions, does our faith have anything to do with the choices we make? The decision to follow Jesus is the beginning of an adventure, full of choices. Sometimes this adventure is called discipleship. Read the texts from Micah and Mark and circle the verbs or phrases that help us understand what is involved with discipleship.

Does your church have a banner or other visual piece that communicates something about discipleship? If so, display this in your meeting area as you work on the Digging Deeper exercises.

Micah 6:8

"He has told you, O mortal, what is good;
   and what does the Lord require of you
but to do justice, and to love kindness,
   and to walk humbly with your God?"

Mark 8:34-35

"(Jesus) called the crowd with his disciples, and said to them, 'If any want to become my followers, let them deny themselves and take up their cross and follow me. For those who want to save their life will lose it, and those who lose their life for my sake, and for the sake of the gospel, will save it.'"

Digging Deeper 2

Study the Confession of Faith Summary with two highlighters (or pencil crayons) in hand. In one color, highlight or underline ideas about what true faith is. In the other color, highlight what true faith is not.

Confession of Faith Summary

We believe that getting to know God will have an impact on how we live our lives in the everydayness: at school, at the party, at the mall, on the team. As we get to know God, we will also get to know Jesus. As we get to know Jesus, we will see that he did an amazing job of living his life every day. We will be drawn to pattern our lives after Jesus—to follow Jesus. This is a two-way street. Getting to know God leads to following Jesus, leads to knowing God better, leads to following Jesus, leads to ... (get it?).

Following Jesus is not something that we accomplish all on our own. God works in us to guide us, help us, and keep us going. "Through grace, God works in us to recreate us in the image of Christ." Here is the two-way street again. Our actions on the outside point to our new birth on the inside which motivate our actions on the outside which point to.... Following Christ includes both salvation and discipleship.

Following Christ may mean choosing a different path than others around you. "True faith in Christ means willingness to do the will of God, rather than willful pursuit of individual happiness. True faith means seeking first the reign of God in simplicity, rather than pursuing materialism. True faith means acting in peace and justice, rather than with violence or military means. True faith means giving first loyalty to God's kingdom, rather than to any nation-state or ethnic group that claims our allegiance. True faith means honest affirmation of the truth, rather than reliance of oaths to guarantee our truth telling. True faith means chastity and loving faithfulness to marriage vows, rather than the distortion of sexual relationships, contrary to God's intention. True faith means treating our bodies as God's temples, rather than allowing addictive behaviors to take hold. True faith means performing deeds of compassion and reconciliation, in holiness of life, instead of letting sin rule over us. Our faithfulness to Christ is lived out in the loving life and witness of the church community, which is to be a separated people, holy to God."

Following Jesus often means making some hard choices. It is not easy to suffer for the right without retaliation. It is not easy to love your enemies. It is not easy to forgive those that persecute you. It was not easy for Jesus, and it is not easy for us. But while following Jesus into the hard choices that may lead to suffering is an important part of the picture, this is not the whole picture. We believe that following Jesus also leads to joy. Sometimes the joy is a feeling, like a bubbling stream. Sometimes the joy comes from knowing you have done a good thing. Joy also comes from our faith that those who follow Jesus along the narrow way that leads to life will indeed live with God.

Respond 1

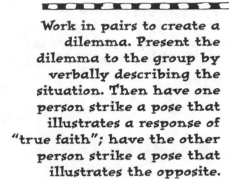

In the second last paragraph of the Confession of Faith Summary, did you highlight eight places where what true faith is is contrasted with what true faith is not? Choose one of these contrasting pairs (i.e., acting in peace and justice rather than with violence). Now create a dilemma (like the scenario in Focus) that illustrates the tension between the two. That is, imagine a situation in which responding in violence would be one option, but responding in peace would be another possibility.

Work in pairs to create a dilemma. Present the dilemma to the group by verbally describing the situation. Then have one person strike a pose that illustrates a response of "true faith"; have the other person strike a pose that illustrates the opposite.

Respond 2

Refer back to the second last paragraph in the Confession of Faith Summary. What would you add to the list of contrasting pairs of what true faith is and is not? Choose pairs that illustrate dilemmas you are facing in your life right now, dilemmas you have faced in the past, or dilemmas you anticipate in the future.

Let youth personalize this list individually. Then create a collective litany by gathering up their ideas and pooling them together. Read this litany aloud, leading into your closing worship time. Could this litany be used in your congregation's worship hour sometime? Be sure to ask permission of the class before you do so.

True faith means _____
    rather than _____
True faith means _____
    rather than _____
True faith means _____
    rather than _____
True faith means _____
    rather than _____

Read aloud the second last paragraph in the Confession of Faith Summary, adding your list before the last sentence.

Closing prayer: In prayer, read the litany you created in Respond 2. Then, celebrate the fact that following Jesus leads to joy! Distribute bottles of bubble liquid. Blow bubbles while singing or telling a story of joyful discipleship. One suggestion: "You shall go out with joy" (Hymnal: A Worship Book, #427).

Closing

Record your personal response to this chapter. What has made an impression on you? What will you remember most? Was anything exciting? What seems most important? Any surprises? Do questions remain? Record your personal response in whatever form you wish: sentences, points, poetry, pictures, music, prayer.

Discipleship and Me

18 CHRISTIAN SPIRITUALITY

Focus

Recall one of the first times you can remember being aware of God's presence. How old were you? What impressions does this memory leave with you?

Explore

What about the time since that early memory? How have you felt connected with God? How have you worked at strengthening that connection? Identify everything in the list below that has helped you connect with God. Circle all that have been a part of your journey.

praying	hearing others pray
making music	listening to music
worship	memorizing Scripture
reading the Bible	studying the Bible
reading books of faith	being alone in nature
helping someone	caring for a child
fasting	living simply
spending time in silence	weathering hard times
sharing deeply with another person	being surrounded by a busy city

Light a candle in your meeting area and place a vine or some other leafy plant beside it. Do this exercise. Offer the opportunity to share memories, but do not insist.

Before class, write each of the activities listed below on slips of paper, one per slip. Pass the stack around the group, inviting each person to (1) choose one thing from the stack that has been a way for him or her to connect with God, and (2) place the slip of paper around the base of the lit candle before passing the stack. If your group is small, give everyone more than one turn.

Digging Deeper 1

Read the text from the Gospel of John for Jesus' description of how we are connected with God. Does the Confession of Faith Summary spark any new ideas about being connected with God?

John 15:5-8

"I am the vine, you are the branches. Those who abide in me and I in them bear much fruit, because apart from me you can do nothing. Whoever does not abide in me is thrown away like a branch and withers; such branches are gathered, thrown into the fire, and burned. If you abide in me, and my words abide in you, ask for whatever you wish, and it will be done for you. My Father is glorified by this, that you bear much fruit and become my disciples."

Confession of Faith Summary

Our lives are full of relationships. All of these connections change and go through stages, and our relationship with God is no exception. God knew us even before we were born. We come to know God more fully all the time.

When we confess Christ and receive baptism, our relationship with God changes. We know God's love in a new way. Our lives are "freed, transformed, reordered, and renewed." We yield ourselves to God. We let the Holy Spirit mold us so that we become more like Jesus. We can also see the Holy Spirit molding the church to become the body of Christ. It is important for individual Christians and whole faith communities to pay attention to their relationship with God.

Observing a grape arbor or an apple tree helps us understand how we are connected with God. A branch cannot live by itself. If it is cut off from the vine or the trunk of the tree, it withers and dies. But when it is connected, it thrives and bears fruit. We draw the life of the Spirit from Jesus Christ, just as the branch draws life from the vine. When we are cut off from the vine, the power of the Spirit cannot reach us, but when we are connected, it fills and fuels us. This connection bears fruit in our lives too. Our behavior on the outside matches our experience of the Spirit on the inside.

How do we stay connected to "the vine?" How can we prepare for times of testing? How do we help our relationship with God to grow? Spiritual disciplines can help us in these directions. Prayer, study of Scripture, acts of service, singing hymns, and other forms of worshipping together are some examples of spiritual disciplines.

We must not forget that all the while we are reaching out for God, God is also reaching out for us. Nothing can separate us from God. Nothing. Not suffering, nor confusion, nor forgetfulness, nor even death. God can use any experience we come up against to strengthen our relationship. And we can look forward to the experience, some day, "when our partial knowledge of God will become complete, and we will see face to face."

Digging Deeper 2

The Confession of Faith suggests that as we come to know God's love, our lives are "freed, transformed, reordered, and renewed" (see the second paragraph in the Confession of Faith Summary). What does it mean to be freed, transformed, reordered, and renewed? What does this feel like? What does it look like? What does it sound like and smell like?

Describe something that illustrates each of these words for you. You may wish to use words or pictures or both. An example for "our lives are freed" could be a bird being released from a cage. What will you come up with?

our lives are freed   our lives are transformed

our lives are reordered   our lives are renewed

Would you say that you have experienced God's love in your life in one of these ways? Circle that one and offer a prayer of thanks.

Which of these experiences of God's love do you yearn for the most right now? Draw a square around that one and offer a prayer of invitation.

Gather four sheets of poster paper, markers, and masking tape. Write one of the words in bold on each sheet of paper as a heading ("freed," "transformed," etc.). Post papers around the room. Distribute markers and let youth circulate around the room, adding their words or pictures to illustrate as many headings as they wish.

Digging Deeper 3

For many, Scripture is an important means of connecting with God, whether in study, prayer, memorization, or reading aloud. Have you ever approached Scripture as a letter written personally to you? In the words of Dietrich Bonhoeffer, "... just as you do not analyze the words of someone you love, but accept them as they are said to you, accept the Word of Scripture and ponder it in your heart, as Mary did. That is all" (*The Way to Freedom*, Harper and Row, 1966). Read Jesus' story of the lost (prodigal) son in Luke 15:11-32. Keep Bonhoeffer's instruction in mind. What does the story say to you?

If time allows, spend a few minutes writing or drawing responses to this question. Otherwise, encourage youth to do this at home.

Respond 1

Have you ever felt intimidated by prayer? Have you ever felt that you want to pray but don't know where to start? It may help to remember that just as people have many different ways of communicating with each other, so are there many different ways of communicating with God.

Distribute one sheet of
paper and a pen per person.
Invite each person to write
a sentence prayer of "praise"
at the top of the page. Now
fold the paper down so the
writing is not visible, and
pass the paper to the right.
This time, add a sentence
prayer of "thanksgiving,"
fold it down, and pass it.
Continue with each of the
five types of prayer. At the
close of the session, unfold
the papers and offer the
prayers together in worship.

Decide together if you will
do this. Will you check in
with each other next time
you meet to see if everyone
followed through?

Origen was an early Christian leader that had some helpful ideas about prayer, even though he was born a long time ago (185 C.E.) and a long way away (Egypt). When we pray, he suggested that we move through five different types of prayers: praise, thanksgiving, confession, petition, and doxology. Try out his approach by composing your own prayer in the chart below (or in your scrapbook if you need more room).

Type of prayer	Definition	Your prayer
praise	acknowledging God's greatness	(Hello, I love you ...)
thanksgiving	thanking God for all God has done and is doing	(Thank you for ...)
confession	acknowledging our sin and asking for healing and forgiveness	(I'm sorry for ...)
petition	praying for others	(Please help ...)
doxology	acknowledging God's greatness in closing	(I love you ... Amen.)

Respond 2

Memorizing Scripture is one way to strengthen our connection with God and invite the Spirit to shape our lives. Choose one of the following Scriptures to memorize:

Luke 11:2-4 (The Lord's Prayer)
Micah 6:8
Luke 10:27
Romans 8:38-39
James 3:17-18

When is a time each day that you could recall this verse and say it to yourself? (For example, when you are getting dressed in the morning, or whenever you ride your bike or take an elevator, etc.)

How will you remember to do it?

Closing

Record your personal response to this chapter. What has made an impression on you? What will you remember most? Was anything exciting? What seems most important? Any surprises? Do questions remain? Record your personal response in whatever form you wish: sentences, points, poetry, pictures, music, prayer.

Christian Spirituality and Me

Closing prayer: Light the candle you used at the beginning of the session and return to the prayers composed in Respond 1. Distribute the prayers and take turns offering them out loud.

19
FAMILY, SINGLENESS, AND MARRIAGE

Focus

Who is a part of your family or household? Who is your church family or household of God? Compare these two families or households. How are your family and your church family similar? How are they different? Jot your ideas below:

how they are different   how they are the same

Explore 1

When it comes to living with people we care deeply about, there's usually two sides to the story. Often there are things we appreciate very much. Often there are things we do not appreciate. Finish the sentences below with your family or household in mind:

On the one hand ...

something I really like is _____

one thing I would never _____
want to change is

On the other hand ...

something I really don't
like is _____

if I could change one thing,
it would be _____

Now return to these questions with your church family in mind:

On the one hand ...

something I really like is _____

one thing I would never _____
want to change is

On the other hand ...

something I really don't like
like is _____

if I could change one thing,
it would be _____

Divide the class into two groups. Ask one group to brainstorm characteristics of the families or households in which they live. Ask the other group to do the same for your church family. Then bring the groups together and sift through their ideas to see how these two families are different and how they are the same. (Since part of this session tries to get youth in touch with different parts of your church family, consider meeting in a primary Sunday school classroom.)

After youth have recorded their ideas, share some of your thoughts and feelings with each other. Go around the circle, inviting each person to share one of their pairs: "On the one hand...," "On the other hand...." Do this first for their families or households, and again for your church family.

Invite a number of people to class, representing a variety of ages and stages of life, to share what it is like for them to be part of the family of God. Invite youth to pose these questions to them and to add questions of their own.

Explore 2

Identify someone in your church family that is at a different stage of life than you are. This may be someone who is married, an older single person, a parent of young children, a senior, or a young adult. Talk with them about their experiences of church life. Use these questions to get you started:

What is your earliest memory of church?

What do you remember about your baptism?

How do you think our church is like a family?

What would you like to change about our church family?

What advice or counsel would you give to youth about being part of a church family?

Digging Deeper 1

What do you think Jesus is saying in the texts below? Write a newspaper headline for each text that succinctly communicates its meaning.

Mark 3:31-35 << _____ >>

"Then his mother and his brothers came; and standing outside, they sent to him and called him. A crowd was sitting around him; and they said to him, 'Your mother and your brothers and sisters are outside, asking for you.' And he replied, 'Who are my mother and my brothers?' And looking at those who sat around him, he said, 'Here are my mother and my brothers! Whoever does the will of God is my brother and sister and mother.'"

Ephesians 1:3-6 << _____ >>

"Blessed be the God and Father of our Lord Jesus Christ, who has blessed us in Christ with every spiritual blessing in the heavenly places, just as he chose us in Christ before the foundation of the world to be holy and blameless before him in love. He destined us for adoption as his children through Jesus Christ, according to the good pleasure of his will, to the praise of his glorious grace that he freely bestowed on us in the Beloved."

Digging Deeper 2

The Confession of Faith Summary communicates a lot of values about family life, children, singleness, marriage, and sex. Are the values stated here consistent with the values you pick up from friends, movies, books, and music? Highlight any values that might be in conflict with what you pick up from your peers or the culture around you. (An example of a value statement is "Single persons should be respected.")

Confession of Faith Summary

We believe that God does not intend for us to be alone. God intends human beings to be connected with each other in loving, supportive relationships. God intends that we will be blessed through families, especially through the family of faith—the church. In the "family of God," everyone has a place, and members treat each other as brothers and sisters. Families of faith are called to be a blessing to all families of the earth.

We recognize that God created each of us as a whole person. Within the church family, it is good to be either married or single. We honor the single state. Single persons should be respected in the church and included in activities of the church family.

"We believe that God intends marriage to be a covenant between one man and one woman for life. Christian marriage is a mutual relationship in Christ, a covenant made in the context of the church. According to Scripture, right sexual union takes place only within the marriage relationship. Marriage is meant for sexual intimacy, companionship, and the birth and nurture of children."

Children are very important. Jesus saw children as examples of how to receive the reign of God. Children are to be loved, disciplined, taught, and respected in their family and in their church family. In turn, children are to honor their parents. Younger people are to respect their elders at home and in the church.

The church is called to help couples build strong marriages and to encourage reconciliation in times of conflict. The church is also to minister to persons in difficult family relationships. The church is called to minister with truth and compassion in such situations. The church is called to offer healing and hope to families, for the church is the family of God.

Reflect on the highlighting you have done. Star (*) any of the values that seem troublesome or challenging to you right now.

Respond 1

Many people in the church believe that there are three good reasons for sexual union: pleasure, closeness, and procreation (having children). Are these good reasons to reserve sex for marriage? Why?

When you consider the theme of sexuality, what other issues emerge that you would like to talk about?

Have you ever asked your parents how they decided whether or not to reserve sex for marriage? Consider having a conversation with one of them about this. Could you also talk with them about other issues you identified? (You might also want to consider other trusted adults as conversation partners: a mentor, Sunday school teacher, sponsor, pastor, or perhaps a family friend?)

Respond 2

Sometimes families experience pain and difficulties. Even happy families aren't always smiling like the families in the minivan commercials on television. Has your family ever received support from your congregation during a time of pain or grief? When was that time?

If a crisis should arise, could you count on your church family for support? What form would you expect that support to take?

How might you be supportive to others in your church family who are experiencing pain and difficulty?

 # Closing

Record your personal response to this chapter. What has made an impression on you? What will you remember most? Was anything exciting? What seems most important? Any surprises? Do questions remain? Record your personal response in whatever form you wish: sentences, points, poetry, pictures, music, prayer.

Family, Singleness, Marriage and Me

Sustain a discussion, drawing on students' work in Digging Deeper 2 and Respond 1. Listen in a nonjudgmental spirit. Speak in love. Probe for places in their lives that could offer support—places that could help them sort through any conflicting values raised here. Talk together about the notion of having a conversation with parents. Is this a good idea?

Open the door for youth to share about issues that are important to them in their families or households. Sustain a discussion if this feels appropriate. Wrap up the discussion with the suggested questions about mutual support in the church family.

Closing prayer: Pray for each other's families. In prayer, take turns naming prayer requests: expressions of thanks, of regret, or of hope perhaps. When a request is named, someone else in the group prays in response to that request. As leader, assume the role of opening and closing the prayer.

20 TRUTH AND THE AVOIDANCE OF OATHS

Focus

Can you recall a time when someone lied to you? What did that feel like? Did your relationship change in any way?

Divide the class into two groups and put the chairs in a circle. Invite one group to sit in the chairs and the other group to sit in the center of the circle. Ask the group in the middle to discuss their response to these questions. After a couple of minutes, ask the group on the outside to summarize what they heard.

Explore

Do you think Jesus wants us to always tell the truth? Why?

Ask the groups to change positions. Again, the group in the middle discusses their response and the group on the outside summarizes what they heard.

Digging Deeper 1

How does the Confession of Faith Summary address the question "Do you think Jesus wants us to tell the truth?"

Confession of Faith Summary

Sometimes people swear oaths as a way of guaranteeing that they are telling the truth. We believe that swearing an oath is not necessary because followers of Jesus should tell the truth in the first place. Jesus told his disciples not to swear oaths, but to let their yes be yes and their no be no. Straightforward. Honest. Whether we are with our families, our friends, at school, or at work, we always carry with us the commitment to tell the truth. When dealing with legal matters, Jesus' followers may simply affirm that their statements are true.

We believe that this teaching also applies to avoiding profane language. Insulting words do not fit very well with speaking the truth in love. Demeaning words do not help build up the body of Christ.

Oaths of allegiance have been used throughout history and are still used today. Governments sometimes ask their citizens to swear oaths of allegiance to show their loyalty to their country or their leaders. As Christians, we believe our first allegiance is to God. When we are baptized, we pledge our loyalty to Christ's community.

Digging Deeper 2

Read the following teaching of Jesus in Matthew:

Matthew 5:33-37

"Again, you have heard that it was said to those of ancient times, 'You shall not swear falsely, but carry out the vows you have made to the Lord.' But I say to you, Do not swear at all, either by heaven, for it is the throne of God, or by the earth, for it is his footstool, or by Jerusalem, for it is the city of the great King. And do not swear by your head, for you cannot make one hair white or black. Let your word be 'Yes, Yes' or 'No, No'; anything more than this comes from the evil one."

Now look at the bigger picture in Matthew 5:21-48. In these verses, there are six times that Jesus says, "You have heard it said..., but I say to you...." In your own words, make a note of the six positive instructions that Jesus gives the disciples in this section:

Section		Jesus' teaching in ...
I	Matt. 5:21-26	vs. 22: _____
II	Matt. 5:27-30	vs. 28: _____
III	Matt. 5:31-32	vs. 32: _____
IV	Matt. 5:33-37	vs. 34: _____
V	Matt. 5:38-42	vs. 39: _____
VI	Matt. 5:43-48	vs. 44: _____

What are your thoughts when you see Jesus' instruction to not swear at all (Matthew 5:34) in the context of all these other teachings?

Respond 1

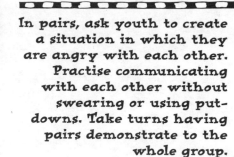

When making choices about how we live, it might seem that the "good" way always means not doing something—in this case, not using profane language. But choices can also be looked at in a positive way. When it comes to the words we use to express ourselves and connect with others, we have lots of choices. We can choose words that speak the truth in love (Ephesians 4:15). We can choose words that build up the body of Christ (Ephesians 4:29). Is it possible to speak the truth in love even when you are angry? How would you do it?

In pairs, ask youth to create a situation in which they are angry with each other. Practise communicating with each other without swearing or using put-downs. Take turns having pairs demonstrate to the whole group.

Respond 2

Imagine that a friend says to you, "Come on, there are so many big problems in the world, why bother getting upset about using bad words?" How do you respond?

Offer someone in the group a microphone to use as a prop. Ask this person to walk around, "talk-show style," posing this question to people at random.

Closing

Record your personal response to this chapter. What has made an impression on you? What will you remember most? Was anything exciting? What seems most important? Any surprises? Do questions remain? Record your personal response in whatever form you wish: sentences, points, poetry, pictures, music, prayer.

Truth and Oaths and Me

Closing prayer: In prayer, read Psalm 19:14. Pray in silence in response to this verse.

21
CHRISTIAN STEWARDSHIP

Focus

Imagine you receive a card in today's mail containing a gift of $100. What will you do with this money?

Explore

How much money is available to you in a month? Write this amount in the middle of the circle below. What happens to this money in a typical month? Where does it go? Divide the circle into wedges according to how it was spent. (i.e., If one third of the money went into clothing, draw a wedge one-third of the circle and label it "clothing.")

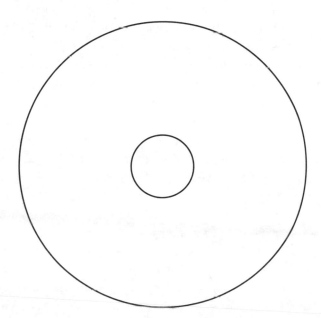

Present each youth with an envelope containing a fake $100 bill. Share what each person would do with this money.

Do this exercise individually, then share what the wedges looked like in each case. Be aware of potential income disparities in your group. Focus on the proportion (i.e., the wedges) rather than the dollars available (i.e., the figure in the center).

Digging Deeper 1

Why do Christians share with others? What motivates us to share our material resources?

Take these questions to the texts below and the Confession of Faith Summary, and note your ideas.

Psalm 24:1

"The earth is the LORD's and all that is in it, the world, and those who live in it."

Mark 12:41-44

"(Jesus) sat down opposite the treasury, and watched the crowd putting money into the treasury. Many rich people put in large sums. A poor widow came and put in two small copper coins, which are worth a penny. Then he called his disciples and said to them, 'Truly I tell you, this poor widow has put in more than all those who are contributing to the treasury. For all of them have contributed out of their abundance; but she out of her poverty has put in everything she had, all she had to live on.'"

Confession of Faith Summary

We believe that everything belongs to God. God has given us new life in Christ. God has given us spiritual gifts. God has given us the good news of the gospel. We can picture God as the head of a household in which we are the servants, or stewards, carrying responsibility for managing the household. We believe that we are to be faithful stewards of all that God has entrusted to us.

God has given us time, to appreciate and use with care. From the earliest days, the people of God were called to set apart special periods for rest and worship. The seventh day, the Sabbath, was one of these. Through Jesus, all time is holy and set apart for God's purposes of "salvation, healing and justice." In our time, the church observes a day of rest and worship, and is called to live according to God's purposes on all days.

In the Old Testament, the years of Sabbath and Jubilee were practical expressions of the belief that everything belongs to God. During these years, land was redistributed, debts were canceled, and slaves were freed. Jesus' ministry is sometimes identified with Jubilee, since through Jesus, the "poor heard good news, captives were released, the blind saw, and the oppressed went free." Early churches put Jubilee into practice by preaching the gospel, healing the sick, and sharing possessions and finances.

Because God has entrusted us with the earth, "we are called to care for the earth and bring rest and renewal to the land and everything that lives on it." Because God has entrusted us with money and things, we are called to live simply, share within the church, work for economic justice, and "give generously and cheerfully." We should not be overly anxious about the necessities of life, but seek first the kingdom of God. "We cannot be true servants of God and let our lives be ruled by desire for wealth."

"We are called to be stewards in the household of God, set apart for the service of God. We live out now the rest and justice which God has promised. The church does this while looking forward to the coming of our Master and the restoration of all things in the new heaven and new earth."

Digging Deeper 2

Identify four principles or values from the material in Digging Deeper 1 that you feel are important. (A "principle" or "value" is an idea that has the potential to shape our actions and decisions.)

1. _____
2. _____
3. _____
4. _____

With these in mind, return to the exercise you did in Explore. Is there anything here you might wish to change? If so, make a note to yourself in the margin.

Invite youth to work on this individually or in pairs. Then share findings with each other by listing the principles and values they identified on the chalkboard or newsprint. Do a cluster of values emerge that are shared by the group?

Respond 1

The word "stewardship" often calls to mind the use of money. But money is not the only part of our lives that is addressed by stewardship. Two other areas are time and gifts or abilities.

If you were to set apart a certain amount of time each week to give to God, what would you do with this time?

If youth desire to implement these ideas, help each other figure out how that might be done. Are there people to talk with? wheels to put in motion? financial support to be explored?

If you identified a certain gift or ability to dedicate to God, what would it be and how would you use it?

Do you desire to make one or both of these offerings a reality? How would you make them happen?

Invite a guest to talk
openly about his or her
financial giving patterns.
Use these questions to get
started.

Respond 2

The Bible has a lot to say about money, but often this is a difficult topic for us to talk about. Take this opportunity to talk with someone about their patterns of financial giving. This may be a family member or someone from your congregation. Here are some possible questions:

When did you start to give?

How do you decide how much to give?

How do you decide where to give it?

Are there any hard issues you face when you are making decisions about giving?

Do you experience joy when you give?

Ask someone to volunteer to
be the person in this
scenario. As a group, work
through this exercise with
this person in mind. If you
have time, do more than one
case study, but do them one
at a time. If you invited a
guest for Respond 3, invite
him or her to stay and
participate in this discussion.

Respond 3

Imagine that you have been saving your money for a long time. Early on, you formed the habit of saving a portion of all the money you earned or were given. You put this money in an account at your bank or credit union, and it collected interest. One day, you are surprised to discover that your savings now total $10,000. You decide it is time to make some decisions about what to do with this money.

Putting yourself in this scenario, respond to the following questions from your own life situation:

What are your long-term hopes and dreams? Do any of these have financial implications?

Do you have any debts or other responsibilities to consider? What are they?

Return to your list of principles and values in Digging Deeper 2. Are any of these relevant to this decision? List the relevant values on the left. On the right, note what each value means for this situation:

Will you consult with anyone else about this decision? Who will that person (or persons) be?

Star (*) any of the questions above that you think would be important for real-life financial decisions you need to make. Are there any other questions you wish to add to the list?

By the way, if the situation above was real, what do you think you would do with the $10,000?

Closing

Record your personal response to this chapter. What has made an impression on you? What will you remember most? Was anything exciting? What seems most important? Any surprises? Do questions remain? Record your personal response in whatever form you wish: sentences, points, poetry, pictures, music, prayer.

Stewardship and Me

Closing prayer: Distribute a ball of clay to each person. Form something that symbolizes what you have to offer God. Place these objects in a box. Ask someone in the group to gift-wrap the box. Place the "gift" on the floor and form a circle around it. Holding hands, dedicate these precious gifts to God in prayer. (Where might this gift box sit after this session as a visual reminder of an attitude of stewardship?)

22 PEACE, JUSTICE, AND NONRESISTANCE

Focus

Imagine that as you are leaving school one afternoon, you come across the school troublemaker beating up somebody. That "somebody" is your best friend. What would you do?

____ stand between them ____ help your friend fight back

____ watch and do nothing ____ use a weapon

____ yell for help ____ call 911

____ other:

Why did you choose the course of action you did?

If your class is small, take turns sharing which course of action each would choose—and why. For a larger class, have people with like choices cluster together and answer the "Why?" question as a group.

Explore

How did Jesus' disciples respond when confronted with a violent (or potentially violent) situation? Can you think of any Bible stories along this line?

Work singly or in groups. Have concordances available to help locate the stories.

Digging Deeper 1

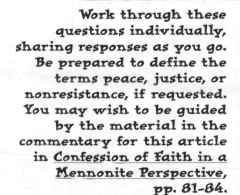

The text from the Gospel of Luke tells of one time when the disciples confronted a violent situation. These are the people involved in this situation:

• Jesus
• police, priests, and elders
• disciple who drew the sword

• Judas
• high priest's slave
• other disciples

Read this text from Luke 22. Which person in the story do you most readily identify with? When you hear the story, whose shoes feel most comfortable?

Work through these questions individually, sharing responses as you go. Be prepared to define the terms peace, justice, or nonresistance, if requested. You may wish to be guided by the material in the commentary for this article in *Confession of Faith in a Mennonite Perspective,* pp. 81-84.

Luke 22:47-54

"While he was still speaking, suddenly a crowd came, and the one called Judas, one of the twelve, was leading them. He approached Jesus to kiss him; but Jesus said to him, 'Judas, is it with a kiss that you are betraying the Son of Man?' When those who were around him saw what was coming, they asked, 'Lord, should we strike with the sword?' Then one of them struck the slave of the high priest and cut off his right ear. But Jesus said, 'No more of this!' And he touched his ear and healed him. Then Jesus said to the chief priests, the officers of the temple police, and the elders who had come for him., 'Have you come out with swords and clubs as if I were a bandit? When I was with you day after day in the temple, you did not lay hands on me. But this is your hour, and the power of darkness!' Then they seized him and led him away, bringing him into the high priest's house."

Read the text from Luke again, but from another person's point of view. Return to the list of the persons involved, and choose someone with whom you didn't readily identify. When you read the account from this person's point of view, did you gain any new insights?

Did the disciple who drew the sword (identified as Peter in other Gospel accounts) have other options? If you had been the disciple, what would you have done?

Post a "graffiti board" in your meeting area and invite youth to write on it the new or striking ideas they find in the article summary. Your graffiti board could be a large piece of table-covering paper, the back of a length of wallpaper, or a piece of drywall. Provide markers in a variety of colors.

Digging Deeper 2

What does the Confession of Faith say about peace, justice, and nonresistance? Read the article summary and underline any striking ideas that are new to you.

Confession of Faith Summary

In the beginning, God created a world of peace. But instead of being content with the world God pronounced "good," humanity chose the way of unrighteousness and violence. Revenge increased. Violence multiplied. But prophets and other messengers of God kept alive a desire to trust in God rather than in weapons and military force. And so, the original vision of peace and justice did not die.

We believe that a commitment to peace was central to Jesus' life; the peace God intended for the world was revealed most fully in Jesus. A joyous song of peace announced Jesus' birth. Jesus taught love of enemies.

He forgave those who did wrong. He called for right relationships. When threatened, he chose not to resist, but gave his life freely. By his death and resurrection, he has removed the dominion of death and given us peace with God.

"As followers of Jesus, we participate in his ministry of peace and justice. He has called us to find our blessing in making peace and seeking justice. We do so in a spirit of gentleness, willing to be persecuted for righteousness' sake. As disciples of Christ, we do not prepare for war, or participate in war or military service. The same Spirit that empowered Jesus also empowers us to love enemies, to forgive rather than to seek revenge, to practice right relationships, to rely on the community of faith to settle disputes, and to resist evil without violence."

We seek to witness to all people that violence is not what God hopes for the world. We believe that God is a God of grace and peace, and we turn to God for help in living lives that reflect these qualities. God guides the church in overcoming evil with good. God empowers us to do justice. God sustains us in the hope of the reign of God—a reign of peace.

Respond 1

Imagine that this diagram records your life. How do you live out these five different aspects of peace in your family, school, church, community, and world? Work on one wedge of the pie at a time, being as specific as possible. For instance, take the "active nonviolence" wedge. I would ask myself, "How do I practice active nonviolence in my family?" I could write down "We don't hit each other" in that piece of the wedge. Then ask, "How do I practice active nonviolence at school? " etc. If you don't have enough space for sentences, use key words.

Before class, reproduce this diagram on a large scale. Cut the pie into wedges. Distribute the wedges to pairs of youth to flesh out. As people finish, post the wedges piece by piece until the pie is complete.

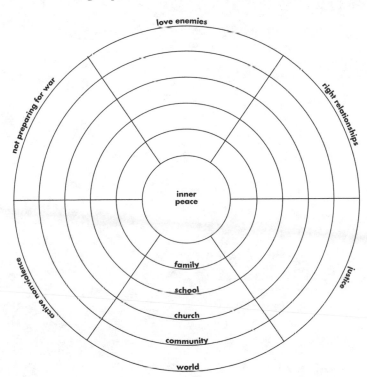

Respond 2

Notice that the center of the pie is the solid piece that touches all of the different wedges. This is "inner peace," or the peace that you experience inside yourself. The deeper this inner peace, the farther the other pieces will extend. The stronger this inner peace, the more likely the other pieces will hang together. How do you nurture the inner peace at your core?

Respond 3

(Optional)

View the video "Ekklesia, Peacemaking: healing and hope," produced in 1995 by Mennonite World Conference and other Mennonite agencies. Looking to followers of Christ in Northern Ireland, India, and Colombia, the video explores the question "How do persons in the peace-church tradition go about being Christ's disciples for justice and peace today?" (Total running time—28 min. Study guide included.)

Closing

Record your personal response to this chapter. What has made an impression on you? What will you remember most? Was anything exciting? What seems most important? Any surprises? Do questions remain? Record your personal response in whatever form you wish: sentences, points, poetry, pictures, music, prayer.

Peace and Me

23
THE CHURCH'S RELATION TO GOVERNMENT AND SOCIETY

Focus

In 1963, Stanley Milgram conducted an experiment in which volunteers were instructed to give an electric shock to the "student" in the next room who was strapped in a chair, attached to an electrode, and given several problems to solve. If you had been one of the volunteers, you would have been told that whenever the student makes a mistake learning a list of word pairs you are to administer a shock—starting with a "slight shock" and increasing in severity with each mistake. You are told that the shocks will be painful for the student, but will not cause any permanent damage. At first the student shows signs of discomfort. Then the student complains. Next the student demands to be released, then screams in agony. You are instructed by the experimenter to continue. How far will you go? Would you go all the way to the maximum voltage, even when you heard no more sounds coming from the student? What would you have done?

> If someone in your group knows of this experiment, let them describe it to the others. Have the group predict what they think the outcome of this experiment would be. To read more about this experiment, see <u>Psychology</u> by Diane E. Papalia and Sally Wendkos Olds, McGraw-Hill, 1985, pages 594-597.

Explore

In Milgram's experiment, the "student" was an actor who only pretended to be receiving shocks. Nevertheless, the act was convincing. Many people would guess that most volunteers would refuse to obey the experimenter at an early point. However, a high proportion of volunteers actually obeyed orders, giving what they thought were painful electrical shocks to another human being. What might this study teach us about obedience? What are your thoughts?

> Was your prediction correct? Share insights about what Milgram's experiment teaches us about obedience.

Digging Deeper 1

Read this account from Exodus. How did the Hebrew midwives understand obedience?

Exodus 1:13-20

"The Egyptians became ruthless in imposing tasks on the Israelites, and made their lives bitter with hard service in mortar and brick and in every kind of field labor. They were ruthless in all the tasks that they imposed on them.

The king of Egypt said to the Hebrew midwives, one of whom was named Shiphrah and the other Puah, 'When you act as midwives to the Hebrew women, and see them on the birthstool, if it is a boy, kill him; but if it is a girl, she shall live.' But the midwives feared God; they did not do as the king of Egypt commanded them, but they let the boys live. So the king of Egypt summoned the midwives and said to them, 'Why have you done this, and allowed the boys to live?' The midwives said to Pharaoh, 'Because the Hebrew women are not like the Egyptian women; for they are vigorous and give birth before the midwife comes to them.' So God dealt well with the midwives; and the people multiplied and became very strong."

Digging Deeper 2

Read the Confession of Faith Summary. Make note of anything that adds to your understanding of obedience—especially obedience to God.

Confession of Faith Summary

(We believe that) "the church is the spiritual, social, and political body that gives its allegiance to God alone. As citizens of God's kingdom, we trust in the power of God's love for our defense. The church knows no geographical boundaries and needs no violence for its protection. The only Christian nation is the church of Jesus Christ, made up of people from every tribe and nation, called to witness to God's glory."

God instituted governments and other human institutions to maintain order in societies. These governing authorities are called to act justly and provide order, as servants of God. "But like all such institutions, nations tend to demand total allegiance. They then become idolatrous and rebellious against the will of God. Even at its best, a government cannot act completely according to the justice of God because no nation, except the church, confesses Christ's rule as its foundation."

We believe that as Christians, we should respect those in authority. We believe that we should pray for all people, including those in government. We seek to be good citizens of the community in which we live, calling for justice, peace, and compassion for all.

Respond 1

What does it mean to be a "good citizen?" Identify three people in your church you would call good citizens. Why did you choose them? To whom are these people obedient, and in what situation?

Divide into groups. Each group agrees on one "good citizen" from the congregation, then answers the two questions in Respond 1. Come back together, and let groups take turns describing the person they chose. Everyone else tries to guess who the person is.

Respond 2

What does it mean to be obedient to God in the situations identified below? Indicate "yes" or "no" beside each one according to your conscience. Would you:

____ hold public office?'

____ vote?

____ join the army?

____ sit on a jury that convicted someone to death row?

____ offer shelter to a refugee who is in your country illegally?

____ other: _____

If there is someone in your congregation with a story to tell about living out obedience to God, invite him or her to class. Leave time for youth to address questions to your guest. Consider breaking the class into pairs or small groups to formulate their questions.

Respond 3

"Justice, peace, and compassion for all." These are qualities we strive to bring about in the communities in which we live. These are also qualities of God's reign that we anticipate in the age to come. What will God's reign look like? What can you do to help move your community in that direction? Draw a picture that captures some of your ideas.

Create a group picture using interesting media: draw a sidewalk mural with colored chalk; paint on an old door; paint a piece of drywall. Consider displaying the finished product on Sunday morning.

Closing

Record your personal response to this chapter. What has made an impression on you? What will you remember most? Was anything exciting? What seems most important? Any surprises? Do questions remain? Record your personal response in whatever form you wish: sentences, points, poetry, pictures, music, prayer.

Church and State and Me

Closing prayer: Lead out with "God, we pray for justice," and invite youth to respond with petitions for justice in your community. Continue with "God, we pray for peace" and "God, we pray for compassion."

24 THE REIGN OF GOD

Focus

What does it feel like to have someone promise you something? Recall a time when a promise was made and kept.

Share these experiences with each other.

Explore

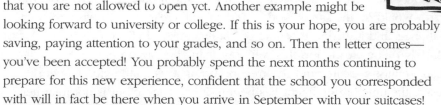

Where in your life is a future hope partially here now, but not yet fully realized? One example might be receiving a wrapped gift that you are not allowed to open yet. Another example might be looking forward to university or college. If this is your hope, you are probably saving, paying attention to your grades, and so on. Then the letter comes—you've been accepted! You probably spend the next months continuing to prepare for this new experience, confident that the school you corresponded with will in fact be there when you arrive in September with your suitcases!

These are just two examples. Can you point to a place in your life where you are waiting for a promise to be fulfilled?

Before class, place the items to be used in Respond 3 inside a box, and wrap the box in festive paper. Use the unopened gift box as a visual aid to communicate the "already but not yet" idea. Be prepared to share an "already but not yet" experience from your own life.

Digging Deeper 1

Many Christians believe that God's reign has a past, present, and a future. To grasp God's reign in the past we can study history. In the present, we can recognize God's reign first-hand. But what about God's reign in the future? What will it be like? When will it come? We have the promise that Christ will come again in glory (among other wonderful things!), but this promise has not yet been fulfilled.

Which seems most important: to *predict* exactly when the coming reign of God will be ushered in, or to *prepare* for that time, whenever it will be? Do the text from Revelation and the Confession of Faith Summary speak to this question? How?

Revelation 21:1-6

"Then I saw a new heaven and a new earth; for the first heaven and the first earth had passed away, and the sea was no more. And I saw the holy city, the new Jerusalem, coming down out of heaven from God, prepared as a bride adorned for her husband. And I heard a loud voice from the throne saying,

'See, the home of God is among mortals.

He will dwell with them as their God;

they will be his peoples,

and God himself will be with them;

he will wipe every tear from their eyes.

Death will be no more;

mourning and crying and pain will be no more,

for the first things have passed away.'

"And the one who was seated on the throne said, 'See, I am making all things new.' Also he said, 'Write this, for these words are trustworthy and true.' Then he said to me, 'It is done! I am the Alpha and the Omega, the beginning and the end. To the thirsty I will give water as a gift from the spring of the water of life.' "

Confession of Faith Summary

In the days of Moses, Aaron, and Miriam, the people of Israel looked to God as their king. They also looked forward to a time when everyone on earth would do the same. God would rule all creation with wisdom, patience, and justice in this time of fulfillment. We believe that God is already ruling creation in this way, but many people do not recognize it. Jesus' ministry, death, and resurrection brought us a little closer—with Jesus, the time of fulfillment has begun. It has begun, but is not fully here yet. When it is complete, God's reign with Jesus as king will be a time of both judgment and healing.

Until God's reign is here completely, it is up to the church to show the rest of the world what it has to look forward to: justice, righteousness, love, and peace, for instance. We believe that the world craves for all of these.

God raised Jesus from the dead, and we believe that someday we will be raised too. When Christ comes again and the time of fulfillment is here, the dead will come out of their graves! Those who walked with God will live with God; those who did not will be separated from God.

We believe that God's reign is something to look forward to. Imagine a new heaven and a new earth where the people of God will no longer hunger, thirst, or cry! Instead, they will sing praises and worship God, a God of justice, righteousness, love, and peace.

Digging Deeper 2

Who will be part of God's kingdom? Perfect people? The ones who have it all together? Who did Jesus say will inherit the kingdom of God? Here are some examples:

Matthew 5:10 _____

Matthew 8:10-12 _____

Matthew 17:20 _____

Matthew 18:3 _____

Luke 6:20 _____

Choose one of these examples and describe what you think it means. For instance, what does it mean to "have faith like a mustard seed"? Use reference books if you wish.

Have available a variety of reference books. Work in pairs to find the references and describe what one of them means. Report findings back to the group. See Appendix 2 for the people to whom these passages refer.

Respond 1

Perhaps you have heard predictions, read articles, or even listened to sermons about the "last days" or the "end of the world." How have these reports affected you? Have they helped to build you up by strengthening your foundation of faith? Have they been confusing? Have they frightened you? Record your thoughts. (Talk with an adult mentor about what you have been hearing. Do not be afraid to ask how he or she puts all this together.)

Lead a discussion guided by these questions. Be attentive to deeply felt concerns, and do not shut down the discussion too quickly.

Respond 2

Showing the world what we have to look forward to in the time of fulfillment is a pretty tall order. Not surprisingly, the church often falls short of this ideal. But have you known moments of the church at its best?

How does your church show love to you?

How does your church extend the hand of peace to your community?

How does your church work for justice?

How does your church model hope for the world?

Work at these prayers individually or in small groups. Indicate that there will be a chance to offer them at the end of class.

Write a short prayer, thanking God for one particular experience of the church at its best—for one glimpse you have had of the reign of God.

Respond 3

As Christians, we believe that in the end, good will win out over evil. Life will conquer death. This is not just the happy ending of a movie; this will be. Really.

Search for an object that symbolizes one of the qualities of God's coming reign, such as love, peace, justice, or righteousness. Place this object someplace in your bedroom where you will see it often. No one else needs to know what it represents to you, but you will see it when you get up in the morning and at other times of the day. When you look at it, remember God's promise that love and life will win in God's final victory.

Closing

Record your personal response to this chapter. What has made an impression on you? What will you remember most? Was anything exciting? What seems most important? Any surprises? Do questions remain? Record your personal response in whatever form you wish: sentences, points, poetry, pictures, music, prayer.

The Reign of God and Me

Have a box full of small items for youth to choose from: pinecones, shells, spools, costume jewelry, balls, beans, nuts, nails, seeds, etc. (If you put these items inside the gift box used in Focus, now is the time to open it.) You do not need to ascribe meaning to these objects—that's their job! Invite everyone to choose two items. Take one item home. With the other, work together to create a group sculpture. You may wire them together, shape a lump of clay and press the items into it, or make a mobile, etc. Decide where the sculpture should stay.

Closing prayer: Lead the group in praying the Lord's Prayer in a responsive manner. As leader, speak one phrase at a time, inviting youth to respond to each phrase with the words "Your kingdom come."
For instance:
Leader: "Our Father"
Youth: "Your kingdom come"
Leader: "Who art in heaven"
Youth: "Your kingdom come," etc.

CLOSING SESSION

Snapshots

What will you remember as highlights of your journey? If you were creating a photo album of memorable moments, what snapshots would be in it? Jot down your memorable moments in the "snapshots" below. Flip through this book and your scrapbook to jog your memory if you wish.

Purchase a small photo album for each person in your group (the kind with "sleeves" for one picture per page). On a sheet of paper, draw rectangles the size of the picture that will fit in the sleeves of the album. Squeeze as many rectangles onto the page as possible. Photocopy this page so that you have at least one page per person. Invite youth to record their memorable moments on the blank "snapshots" you have given them, and have them sign each one. While they are working on the next exercise, photocopy their snapshots (as many copies as you have people), cut them apart, and collate one album for each youth. Result: identical albums, one for everyone to take home.

What Are Your Co-ordinates?

Where has your journey taken you? Where do you find yourself now?

Are you at the same place you were when you began, or someplace different?

What do you find underfoot where you are now? solid rock, mucky swamp, shifting sand, something else

What is the weather like where you are now?

What is the landscape like around you? mountainous, prairie, woodland, coastal, other

If there was a signpost where you are now, what would it say?

Sketch a picture that depicts where you are now. Title it with a word or two that communicates how you feel about being in this place.

Where Did You Hope to Be?

Turn back to the Destination exercise in the Opening Session, p. 2. Copy below the goals you identified at the beginning of this journey:

I hoped to _____

I planned to _____

I wished _____

I aimed to _____

Have your hopes come to be? Reflect on where you are now in relation to where you hoped to be when you began.

How Would You Sum Up Your Travels?

Skim over the sessions again, looking this time for points that could be included in a personal testimony: elements of faith that are foundational for you, key insights, cutting-edge questions, etc. Pay special attention to any journaling you did at the end of each chapter. Now write your testimony.

Share these testimonies with each other.

Where Are You Headed?

Reaching the end of this book may feel like a milestone, but it is certainly not the end of your journey of faith. If some of the goals you identified at the beginning have not been met, are there ways to continue working at them? If seeking baptism was not one of the goals you identified, are you open to exploring this possibility? (If so, who would you talk to about this?) Where will your journey take you next? Respond to as many of these questions as you wish.

Bring out the backpack again. Pass it around the group. Ask whoever is holding the backpack to "think out loud" about where their journey of faith is headed. Some may have clear ideas already. All may benefit from having the group focus on them to probe the possibilities.

Share these testimonies

Close your time together
with celebration and
fellowship (including food!).
Bring a camera, take a group
picture, and get reprints
later for youth to add to this
session's photo album or
their scrapbook. As a sending
prayer, sing #429 in Hymnal:
A Worship Book, or some
other "youth-friendly"
doxology. Go in peace.

Sending

Find a way to celebrate your arrival at this milestone of your journey. What would feel appropriate: taking your pastor out for ice cream and sharing parts of your experience with him or her; sharing something at your next youth group meeting or Sunday school class; doing something active with your mentor or whoever you identified in the Opening Session as your traveling companion?

Wherever your journey takes you next, may this prayer go with you:

"Go now in peace,
May the love of God surround you,
Everywhere you may go."
(*Hymnal: A Worship Book*, #429)

Appendix 1
Answers to Exercises

Chapter 1: God
Focus
All are images of God found in the Bible:

Genesis 49:24 (rock)

Isaiah 63:1 (water)

Psalm 18:2 (shield)

Psalm 23 (shepherd)

Isaiah 66:13 (mother)

Malachi 1:6 (father)

Isaiah 33:22 (ruler)

Psalm 7:11 (judge)

Hosea 13:8 (mother bear)

Chapter 4: Scripture
Focus
All nine statements are true.

1. Judges 15:4-5
2. Leviticus 19:27
3. Acts 5:17-19
4. Genesis 5:32
5. Acts 12:21-23
6. 1 Kings 18:38
7. Isaiah 8:1, 3
8. Amos 9:3
9. Judges 10:1; 2 Samuel 23:9; 2 Samuel 23:24

Chapter 15: Ministry and Leadership
Explore

Story 1: discernment

Story 2: accountability

Story 3: call

Digging Deeper 2

2 Timothy 4:1-3	speak divine truth with boldness
Matthew 9:35-37	relate with compassion to the needy
1 Timothy 4:13	interpret the Scriptures and the faith diligently
Philippians 2:1-4	lead the congregation in faithful living
Titus 2:15	preach and teach with authority
Ephesians 4:11-13	equip the saints

Chapter 16: Church Order and Unity
Respond 1

In keeping with the material in this chapter, the writer acknowledges that some may rate these items differently than she did. For herself, she rated the first two items on the list always, the last two items never, and everything in-between sometimes.

Chapter 24: The Reign of God
Digging Deeper 2

Matthew 5:10	the persecuted
Matthew 8:10-12	the outcasts
Matthew 17:20	those who have faith like a mustard seed
Matthew 18:3	those who are like children
Luke 6:20	the poor

Appendix 2
Materials Needed

Note: All chapters assume that youth have access to the materials noted in the Opening Session.

Opening Session
- for each person (including yourself) you will need the following: an inexpensive backpack, a copy of this book, a scrapbook (a three-ring binder with blank and lined paper, and dividers if you wish), a copy *of Confession of Faith in a Mennonite Perspective*, and a collection of pencils, pens, and markers
- ensure that each person has a Bible
- letter-sized envelopes
- paper
- pens and pencils

Chapter 1
- an object to represent each of the following: rock, water, shield, shepherd, mother, father, ruler, judge, mother bear
- hearts cut from red construction paper, two per youth
- pipe cleaners, chenille wire, clay, or some other moldable material

Chapter 2
- microphone (for use as a prop; does not need to be "live")

Chapter 3
- chalkboard and chalk or poster paper and markers
- large piece of fabric
- fabric paints
- copies of *Hymnal: A Worship Book* (or whatever hymnal your congregation uses)
- a bowl of GORP ("Good Ole' Raisins and Peanuts") or some other high-protein snack
- reflective music, live or recorded (optional)

Chapter 4
- statements from Explore written on slips of paper (i.e., 8 1/2" by 11" sheets of paper cut in quarters)

Chapter 5

- slips of paper (i.e., 8 1/2" by 11" sheets of paper cut in quarters)
- pencils
- basket
- a variety of craft supplies and materials
- POSSIBLE GUEST: someone to help with craft in Respond 1

Chapter 6

- nutritious snack, such as crackers, cheese, fruit
- chalkboard and chalk or poster paper and markers

Chapter 7

- newspapers and news magazines
- poster paper
- scissors
- glue
- markers
- hymnals

Chapter 8

- statements from Explore written on slips of paper (i.e., 8 1/2" by 11" sheets of paper cut in quarters)
- basket
- poster paper
- markers of various colors
- GUEST

Chapter 9

- 8' length of newsprint roll
- large pieces of construction paper in various colors
- scissors
- glue
- blank prescription sheets
- pens
- video: "Ekklesia: witnessing to Christ in today's world"

Chapter 10

- one candle per person
- one sturdy candle that will stand on its own
- matches
- unsalted popcorn
- salt and other popcorn flavorings (cheese powder, chili powder, etc.); or different flavors of potato chips, including unsalted

- "Vision: healing and hope" bookmarks
- overhead transparencies
- permanent markers
- hymnals

Chapter 11

- the vessels your congregation uses for baptism (i.e., pitcher, towel, basin, etc.)
- GUEST

Chapter 12

- whole-grain bread
- grape juice
- small glasses
- candles
- matches
- recorded music (optional)

Chapter 13

- towel
- basin with water
- GUEST
- hymnals

Chapter 14

- newsprint and markers or chalkboard and chalk
- hymnals

Chapter 15

- two bells or buzzers (optional)
- slips of paper (i.e., 8 1/2" by 11" sheets of paper cut in quarters)
- pens and pencils

Chapter 16

- small table
- large cardboard box prepared as instructed
- bed sheet
- ladder (optional)
- slips of paper (i.e., 8 1/2" by 11" sheets of paper cut in quarters)
- pens and pencils
- basket
- strips of paper of different colors (about 1.5" by 8.5")
- tape

Chapter 17

- a banner or other visual piece that communicates something about discipleship (optional)
- highlighters or pencil crayons in various colors
- bubble liquid and bubble wands
- hymnals

Chapter 18

- candle
- matches
- vine or other leafy plant
- four sheets of poster paper
- markers
- masking tape
- paper
- pens and pencils

Chapter 19

- GUESTS

Chapter 20

- microphone (for use as a prop; does not need to be "live")

Chapter 21

- envelope containing fake $100 bills (one per person)
- modeling clay or play dough
- gift box
- wrapping paper
- tape

Chapter 22

- large piece of newsprint roll, old wallpaper, or a piece of drywall
- markers or paints in a variety of colors
- a large copy of the diagram in Respond 1, cut into wedges
- brightly colored construction paper
- scissors
- glue
- video: "Ekklesia, Peacemaking: healing and hope"

Chapter 23

- GUEST
- sidewalk and sidewalk chalk, an old door or piece of drywall and paints

Chapter 24

- a variety of small items, such as pinecones, shells, spools, costume jewelry, balls, beans, nuts, nails, seeds, etc.
- box
- wrapping paper
- tape
- material to connect items in a sculpture or mobile: i.e., wire, lump of clay, dowel rod, and string, etc.

Closing Session

- a small photo album for each person in your group (the kind with "sleeves" for one picture per page)
- paper
- scissors
- access to photocopier
- crayons, markers, paints or oil pastels
- sealed envelopes prepared in Opening Session
- backpack from Opening Session
- camera
- celebration food
- hymnals

Appendix 3
Planning for Guests and Other Special Events

Guests and special events will greatly enhance your time together, but they require forethought. Making arrangements well in advance will save time and frustration.

Guests

Early in your time together, ask youth for a short list of persons whose faith journeys would interest them. Remember these suggestions as you make arrangements for invited guests:

Chapter 5: You may wish to invite someone to prepare and lead the creative expression part of this session.

Chapter 8: Invite someone willing to be interviewed by your class around the general question "What has salvation meant to you?" More specific questions will be composed during class time. Give the guest a copy of this session beforehand so he or she knows the context from which the questions will come, but be sure this person understands that the questions will not all be available ahead of time.

Chapter 11: Invite someone to share their baptism story.

Chapter 13: Invite a guest to respond to the question "What does foot washing mean to you?" This could be an older person who may remember various ways the congregation has practised foot washing.

Chapter 16: Invite a staff member from your conference or district to visit you. Talk with the staff to learn about their work, their vision for the church, and the challenges they face. Work at understanding how your congregation fits into a larger network of congregations.

Chapter 19: Invite a number of people to class who represent a variety of ages and stages of life to share what it is like for them to be part of the family of God. Provide these guests with a copy of the questions listed in Explore 2, and alert them that youth may wish to ask other questions as well.

Chapter 23: Invite someone in your congregation with a story to tell about living out obedience to God. Ask this person to be prepared to tell his or her story and then answer questions from the group.

Videos

Chapter 9: "Ekklesia: witnessing to Christ in today's world," produced in 1992 by Mennonite World Conference and other Mennonite agencies. The video is a window into different ways of being the church around the world. (Total running time—28 minutes. Study guide included.)

Chapter 22: "Ekklesia, Peacemaking: healing and hope," produced in 1995 by Mennonite World Conference and other Mennonite agencies. Looking to followers of Christ in Northern Ireland, India, and Colombia, the video explores the question "How do persons in the peace-church tradition go about being Christ's disciples for justice and peace today?" (Total running time—28 minutes. Study guide included.)

Other

Chapter 10: Order "Vision: healing and hope" bookmarks from your denominational office. Distribute them at the end of class.

Chapter 16: Instead of inviting a conference or district staff person to your class, consider visiting the offices of your conference or district as a group.